RIPPLES ON THE SURFACE

Katmoran Publications ®
www.katmoranpublications.com
Bolton, MA 01740

Copyright 2006 by Franki deMerle
www.reincarnationbooks.com

ISBN: 978-1-939484-07-9

Second Edition 2013
First Edition 2006

Reading this volume of poems by Franki deMerle is an active, generative experience that immerses me in the question of what a poem is. *Ripples on the Surface* is not surface material; it is the tide of meaning itself. The poems question creativity, longing, love, courage, sacredness, and other themes well known to poetic reflection. This questioning is invitational to reflection and the reader should be warned the possible conversations within self that emerge could be dangerous. I did not have the sense so much of reading while immersed in these poems as I had my mind open to poetic experience. Be ready to feel, hold confusion, honor longing, greet isolation, uncover the hidden, and bare the soul.

The strong theme concerns love and the courage to be. This ranges from an existential knowing that "I've chosen who I am" (poem 125) to the challenge to "Be what you want to be" (poem 155). DeMerle effects honesty in exploring isolation and hiddenness that manages brilliantly to ripple through the surface to touch the imagination of the reader and emerge as anything but isolation or hiddenness.

Franki DeMerle, the poet, has a natural knowing of dream symbols and human development. What she does so well that touches the place of poetry in the tradition of personal grounding for human experience is the naming of "Dream Shine" (see poem 131). The dream shine encourages the reader to be poetic if not in verse then no less in *being-ness* as a journey of the human that has always marked our Western Minds.

These 289 poems extend beyond their count to a vast space of aliveness. I trust you will value them. - James Max Gossett, PhD

Franki deMerle's poetry collection "Ripples on the Surface" is, on first reading, a journey that leads the reader in a broad exploration of deep personal feelings, experiences, and life-concepts that connect us to her unique personhood by way of our shared awareness, dreams, longings and losses.

But it was in the second reading that I found myself drinking more deeply from the well of larger thoughts and emotions that unite us all as human beings with all our hopes, doubts, imperfections, illusions, and unexplored depths. And that is what gave this reader the most to ponder about as the message of the book.

The ability to give and receive love is the most prominent theme throughout the collections. Related topics of courage, loss, childhood, friendship, and the unspeakable mysteries of life and of the spirit do indeed ripple through Franki's poetry in a sensitive eloquence, revealing her true and affirming use of language as a window into the heartfelt music of her soul. - Jennifer Pratt-Walter, poet, composer, harpist.

Each poem captures a moment of realization. These little songs seem very personal, but they speak the emotions of every human heart. - Vancouver, WA.

Ripples on the Surface: They just made me feel hopeful, sad, sentimental, strong...inspired. Each piece allows me to envision something new. - Donna Cavanagh, poet, founder of HumorOutcasts.com, and author of Try and Avoid the Speed Bumps.

RIPPLES ON THE SURFACE

Franki deMerle

1.

Beneath the night sky clandescence
An abstract vagueness of unfamiliarity
No focal point for reference
No apparent pattern
Just echoes in the gloom
That wondrous experience
Of something new

*

2.

Coldness, winter and a little day
Rhythms merge as evening wanes
Cluttered in a little space
Spending paper, shedding haste

I marvel at each new pattern
That comes like the others from one inner pulse
I wonder what sounds inside each head
How some beats are words and some science meant

I think of the energy
So well harnessed in each pulse
And wonder at the peaceful love
Created by such force

*

1

3.

We're drawn to the light
Moth to the flame
Ego into spirit purified

To forgive is to let go
Of the pain
That binds us in this world

Loneliness and tears
Rejection and fears
Lost in the simplicity of the moment

*

4.

My home is built of paper words
So easy to tear down, erase, burn
My house is painted with a pen
Windows and doors slowly sketched in

To give you a foyer into my life
To build a dreamer's bed for us to share
Within the circle of my words and your eyes

*

5.

My love is my value
My being is a mine for the jewels that are yours
The strength that is ours
The kindness that is power
The thought that is love

*

6.

Wilderness is a maze
Of misunderstandings
Trying desperately to understand

Contentment
Lies buried and hidden beneath the lies
That most don't realize are there

In the mid of night
Search for the other side of your life
Stand face to face with all other faces

Realize
That out of all the countless places
You have chosen to be here

*

7.

All the odious schedules and times
Of appointments, arrivals, departures and flights
Bore me past despondency
I simply will arrive

*

8.

Sensitivity in a concreted-over world
Dark smut covers the landscape at times
Dusts the heart of every bleeding wood but yours
Yours has survived a cataclysmic world
Tender and bruised and ever good
To give flow to the color of peace in your face
To reach out—to give
And take only love
Love mid abuse
And love amid trials that bear no sentence
Jury and judge await the forgiveness of you

The sensitive leaf folds when touched
Backs off from mockery
Gently blushes from kindness
Curls its many fingers to grasp
Miming the palms of a child in cautious curiosity
It sways with the breeze and bends with the storm
But from the cruel ax it does not flinch
Does not relinquish its grasp of light
But gives up life instead

The way of justice in the earth is strange
Seems unfair if not explained
That some should live so long
Others die so young
Some defy death til all blooming is done
As your father uncurled his caution and blood
To share and pass on
To eternalize the young
He imposed on the world a moment of good
And showered the earth above which he stood
With a soft snow of pink

The veil of the aging
A gift to remember or press between pages
Of all his life's works summarized in beauty
As if glimpsing in secrecy renewal of all life
And after the petals had long fallen away

And crackling brown pods had crumbled away
The world closed its eyes for the birth from a seed
Of you

*

9.

There's a magic in silence
The magic of now
Hidden in stillness
A mysterious presence all around

Revealed in experiencing now
Like a child awakening
Discovering consciousness

*

10.

Fragments of clouds drift and separate
Marking night sky with memories
Fading segments swirl into black

And stir the memory of forgotten dreams
That tell what has been and what is forthcoming
Wrestle the black and then burst at the seams

Whatever floats by in the sky of the evening
Passes on
And I wonder just what it will mean

*

11.

Love can only stumble
In the pettiness of definitions
Listen with the heart
Not with the foolish mind
Toss the words aside
And find the meaning deep inside

*

12.

Our lives are conglomerates of dependencies
We haven't the power to turn ourselves green
So we let the sun turn us brown

Such a confused race
With cultures of contradictions
And bungling ways

We can see but don't often look very far
And for all our religions of brotherly love
We seem to think saving ourselves is enough

And in the chaos of charitable wealth
We lose the naïve trying so hard to help
They don't have time to save themselves

From the sudden degradation
And disintegration
Of realizing nobody cares

*

13.

My room is a cobweb
And my life is a maze with no direction
So I wander the dark halls
And feel the cold space with my hands clenched
But you have come to me
Though lost in illusion I have friendship
As I wander I look through your eyes
And see mirrors of jewel spun webs

And in the darkness
I feel you beside me
And my fingers open like flower petals
To hold your hand

*

14.

Truth is evasive
Advice effervescent loses its shine
All too soon
Words slip away into sound

Everyone has to find themselves
And look inside from without
And I realize all I've said and done
Was only for myself

Could it be the emotion
You see in another
Is the mirror image
Of what you hate—

What you don't want to be
What you know you are
What you're afraid
To face and change?

*

15.

Sleeping limbs quiver
Under minimal weight
Of migrating folding wings

A pine shivers
The sun shimmers out of sight
A solitary blackbird sings

Lost in the blackening sky
A meteorite shower passes by
Condensation materializes

Once again the sun rises
Burns away the veil
And I realize I linger
In the well of a passing moment

*

16.

Perception progresses from the outward senses
Into the depths beyond physical being
And initiates breakdown and elimination
Of barriers

Something turns inside
Senses distracted, unaware
A surge of escape
Rejuvenation

Expelled into another somewhere else
Total expression
Communication with all that is
Absent of pride and inhibition

And nothing is ever the same after that
Expansion of boundaries
You see yourself in a wave passing by
And wave back

*

17.

Life is the teacher of all there is
What to do, what to say, how to live
I don't need experiments or essays
To listen
Bitterness and tension are superficial
Love is natural

Is it hard to cope with other people
To respect their feelings good and evil
Humans cannot survive alone
All plants and animals interrelate
And spirits do not know the boundaries
Bodies make

*

18.

Thought paints the world
In the colors we feel
Ther we try to talk
Of what we think is real

Insecurity condemns
Confidence tells the truth
To be understood
We resort to words

Words are mortal
But words can eliminate possibility
Or heighten anticipation
Or define a distance between me and you

Words can close minds
Or open eyes to incredible views
Our tools
Expressions of awareness

But words are not the person
Just definitions of happiness
Being one in sheer existence with love
Is consciousness

*

19.

Senses awaken
Cells enlivened
Living perception
Of the moment
Of the present
Awareness of divine creation
And microscopic evolution
Transformation now

Animal senses perceive appearances
But one vision experiences
Where there is duality is relativity
Laughs in the darkness
And shines through the night

Citizens of eternity
Traveling wave harmonics
Waking to awareness of each other
Inseparable
Together in the same orbit
Comets falling into the sun
One vibration set into motion
By a dream

*

20.

I went to meet my former self
We stood there face to face
As if I stood upon the grave
In which I had been laid

The garden blossomed from the well
That vast expanse of mind
And as the gardener watched and smiled
I smelled the peace of thyme

And healed the sore so deep a wound
The shock of realizing
All I had been taught was true
Was falsely theorizing

Man-made church, man-made God
Lacking inspiration
But to know the truth at last
Is just compensation

And comforting to feel again
My feet upon the path
That led me safely to myself
And claim my right to laugh

*

21.

Life is a flicker
The balance that brought us here
Now brings us together

Someone lit a candle
And you are holding the match

*

22.

We all have fantasies and greed
And need to suffer the results of mistakes
We all have the ability
To look a stranger in the eye
And say what we have done
Tolerance is difficult to find its place
To know the difference
Between wrong and mistakes

*

23.

An outsider at social gatherings
Looking for humanity
What is wrong with society
That it doesn't take time to be kind?

Alone and alienated
Fearful and frustrated
What is wrong with me
That I take myself seriously?

Understanding has failed
The sensitive are shunned as daft
It seems there is no alternative
But to laugh

*

24.

Those that would deceive
Perceive vulnerability
Instead of strength
And are deceived
We must never be impatient
With those who mourn
For bodies that keep changing
In size and form

We are all wounded
We've all hurt each other
By demand
It's time the wounds were mended

We create sorrow to learn compassion
And experience tenderness
In seeking understanding of others
We learn ourselves instead

*

25.

Curiosity of the morbid
Photographing despair
Why are we so magnetized by destruction?
Why do we stare?

Like watching a log burn in the fireplace
Try to take your eyes away
Something inside is calmly reassured
That all must pass away

*

26.

The homeless merely seeking shelter
From the rain that washes their names down the gutter
Flit about in search of food
Like pesky flies lighting on crumbs
Unidentified and misunderstood
The tree of society is slowly uprooted

Most churches these days
Lock their doors at night
For fear of being looted

*

27.

Everyone acts out their dreams
Whether they are aware
Regardless of what's imposed on me
I am only what I have come to believe
Through experience and dreams

*

28.

The only time you can claim your shadow
Is when the daylight fades
So I made a pact with the devil
To unite in twilight haze

Now I look around
The light surrounds
With shadows nowhere to be found

The light is in me
The darkness free
Shadows nowhere to be seen
But formless energy

You can only create your shadow
With your own density

*

29.

She's afraid
Cause she thinks she doesn't know the rules
Doesn't understand cause and effect
Feels left out
Trying to fit in
And always must pretend

We find it so hard to say
I don't know
We think it demeaning to admit
I don't know
But life is baffling
And people uncanny
And I don't know

How to fit in—
Gave up long ago
Why pretend
I just don't know

*

30.

There's a voice that speaks
Beyond wavelengths
Of satellites and TVs

There's a hum in the wind
Not meant for me
But I heard anyway

There is no death
There is nonacceptance of reality
But upon awakening

There is strength of love
Withstanding
Greater than all hate can conceive
Because where
Is more bitter
If bitterness exists

*

31.

Bright red clays beside red waters
Amid green implications
Leave me feeling a little disappointed
By material domination

But the greenery whispers to linger a moment
And feel the touch of red sand
And as the mud settles down under the water
I feel stranded in a crowded land

*

32.

Measure intelligence by IQ
Measure creativity by what's produced
Measure wisdom by truth

*

33.

To be something else
You have to change yourself
Restlessness isn't ready
To solve the problem
Complaining only wants
To be accepted

Be kind
As if the fault is your own
Be mindful
The thought of wrong is your own

*

34.

Used to be a home
Fallen and crumbled
A sharecrop family shed

Now vines overgrown
Cover its secrets
As a child I found treasure there

A small book of illustrations
Breres Fox and Bear
Drawn by one who couldn't write

I saved it
And tucked it away in a drawer
But my mother threw it away

*

35.

The darkest hour
Is intense trivia
By leisure, by will
Sings like an aria

For all the dissonant words we spill
We have the power
To blend together in one grand trill
And unexpectedly encounter
Unison

*

36.

When you are silent
And when you speak to me
When you look at me
And when you turn away
I exhale and inhale
A bit of you into me

I was confused
And you were kind
I gave you a minute
And you gave me time

*

21

37.

I thought I was over you
But I want you back now
When everything's going wrong
That's when I loved you wasn't it
When everything went wrong

Just a passing memory
Everything that went wrong for us
I still care in a quiet way
And I cry realizing
I'll never hold your hand again

*

38.

Will fulfills imagined ideals
But concrete desires interfere with health
Stop wanting
Start having
Will arouses energy
Which materializes

*

39.

Looking at other faces
Sometimes I find one that reminds me of you
And all we found to be true

Truth doesn't change
But when you're not inside it
There are many different views

I've lived through many transformations
Life has filtered the complications
And lowered many expectations

And of all the choices we have made
I do what hurts the least
I died the day you turned away

You taught me how to laugh again
You taught me to enjoy humanness
You taught me how to live

You never came back
You didn't write back
Good thing you taught me to forgive

*

40.

Years of action had passed
And I thought you were just another person
That I didn't know
Until suddenly the face I had hardly noticed

Glanced familiarly back at me
And in one of those seconds in which I passed by
I recognized you
Too late

*

41.

Will you not tell me
What troubles your eyes?
Is there nothing I can do
To put light into your eyes?

Ours was a relationship of misunderstandings
So undefined that I never knew
When it began or ended
And for all I know still endures
In passing

I wonder if we will ever again
Exchange thoughts someday

*

42.

Watch the sun set
Close the book on that chapter of life
Remnants of past inner conflicts
Flicker by
Hoping to be extinguished

In the newfound void of night
Sleep and rest
Let time pass by
Savor the freshness of the blank page
Before beginning the next phase of life

*

43.

We carry our habits
Wherever we go
In case we need them
As if all we do
Depends upon them

In the end
They flash before us
The strongest guide us
To where we will go

*

44.

The toy's eyes were broken
Tubes that once lit up with sound
The voice of a people
Disguised in the eyes of a dog

The lake as it ripples disturbs the faces
Stars shining through to the surface from below
As I float along and try to touch them
They part through my fingers in the dark below
With memories I find light to seek them out again

The bottom of the lake eludes me in my balance
With the ripples on the surface
Does the sand stir below
Or are they clouds dispersing from a meeting long ago

The ripples part in circles
And die only on dry shores
But flickers as the circles pass
Haunt from their dark abyss
As the brightest stars don't dare betray their distance

Eyes familiar to me draw
With rivers deeper than this
Draw me inward into stars
Above, before, beyond
And I do not know to dive deeper or to swim

There are cities in the sand and coral
Places I have acted in
Are flooded in the present stream
Of spirals rising for tomorrow

Why can't I touch the memories
Or hold the waters of a friendship's place
Within my groping hand
That wants to touch the faces
Burn its fingers on remembered stars
That died in the darkness of a fallen land

*

45.

Life and love
The interchanging gifts
Through all eternity coexist

When suffering
All you need to know
Is that there is life that loves you

*

46.

Memories of a time and place
Where the colors were so vibrant
And spirits were so free
Almost vanished without a trace

Memories of the chasm of fear
Like a dangling rope remaining
From a battered bridge of hope
Almost wiped out by the years

Once an entry on a disk
Brilliant dreams and abilities
Erased to make more space
Put away beyond common access

And over the years what has been learned
Gave meaning to beauty once taken for granted
Waiting for the key to freedom
Searching for pieces to put back together

Once in my youth I knew heaven
But the world led me far away
Now I savor the sensation of long buried treasure
As I search for the gate to the garden

*

47.

Life is often sarcastic
It makes us the spectator
It makes us the centerpiece
It places us in competition
And demands we work together
So I bicker with Fate and Fortune
In the end I will have my own way

*

48.

Like a climax remembered past the ending scene
The play goes on after the curtain is drawn
Somewhere else

Truth doesn't know the boundaries of time
It's as much alive in dreams
As hindsight

*

49.

I don't know where I'm going anymore
Can you tell me
Where is it we've been?
Where is a place or time that exists
Other than within?

*

50.

Feeling small
Snowflake fallen
In all of winter

*

51.

A poem is a personal thing
It speaks individually to anyone who reads
And finds a personal message there
In that the poet cared

I choose to share my thoughts with you
Exposing feelings to outside scrutiny
People often jump to conclusions
And misinterpret what they read

I choose to risk rejection
And open my soul for inspection
Trusting your sensitivity
That you at least will care

But mostly in our daily lives
We laugh at feelings exposed
Or become annoyed at the audacity
That one might be so bold
To speak directly to the heart
Things not usually told
In the company of others
As if we are alone

Spirit imprisoned in human form
Feeling safely clothed
By a body covering up
The nakedness of the soul

*

52.

This is a letter in a bottle
From one stranded in a sea of people
On a deserted listening post

Thousands have chosen solitude
In order to better communicate
With someone higher up

I am among the world-weary
Things never work out as hoped
And so I've given up

But when you give up pain and sorrow
It frees your hands to reach for tomorrow
Or hold on to the moment

The mystic sees in riddles
And writes down as poetic verse
What others have already learned

Mistrust comes from intimacy breached
Rejection and exposure to humiliation
Lead to withdrawal and renunciation

Here I am
Trying desperately
To understand

*

53.

Saw an old friend in the grocery store
Poetry sorting through the cans
Infinite name brands

What an incredible freedom we have
To choose what we eat
To eat what we like

What an incredible being we have
To choose what to be
To be what we might

*

54.

All is good in the beginning
A babe in the cradle of life
Knows only present feelings
The moment satisfied

Life is not disappointed
With any given birth
Life does not anticipate
It knows its innate worth

We are part of its creation
This none dare deny
Expression of pure feeling
Does not tell a lie

And if I reach into a heart
Must not devalue what I see
Any may stab me in the dark
But not manipulate me

For that would be a losing game
Pretending boundaries
And only those may play
That have chosen to believe

*

55.

Language is a marvelous thing
But there are minds where there are no brains
And we have been lost in translation

In what language does the wind speak
That carries the essence of creation?

*

56.

Little voices
Lots of loving
Lots of energy
Ever caring
Always learning
Copying all they see

Once upon a time
I saw rainbows in the sky
The clouds could dance
The sun would shine
And all the world was mine

Once I had a little friend
I shared his world and time
But because he was my friend
I could not call him mine

Voices bubbling
Always singing
Mostly out of tune
Ever sharing
Always bringing
Something bright and new

Once upon a time
I saw rainbows in the sky
My heart could dance
The sun shone bright
And all the world was mine

Once I thought to be a flower
And hold all life within
Perhaps someday my heart will bloom
And life might live again

*

57.

In fantasy the pieces fit
The picture's whole and perfect
But reality is fragmented
I write poetry to pretend

And that's the connection
The bridge over duality
To a place of light and beauty
Where love is real

*

58.

From under curtained strands
Covering ornaments
Blue shadows light's hands of
Orange sparkles
Mountain sprays fall
In splashing columns
Cooled into silent ripples
Washed in a bronze hall
Never by a shore at home

*

59.

I search because my vision blurred
Such fuzziness to sort out
I grope for light and direction
There's so much to wonder about

If I could see clearly
I wouldn't have to search
Lacking sensibility
I stumble in finding words

Discarded dissension
Is division
Unison is made
Of harmonic dimension

But lack of sleep is depressing
It makes you forget who you were
And lack of dreams is oppressive
It makes the whole world hurt

*

60.

What kind of beings are we
That we have invented language
We cannot use to explain all we are?
What other creatures by communicating so much
Create a communication barrier?

*

61.

The bird flies into the mirror
Knocks itself silly
Doesn't know the difference
Numb from pain
Disoriented by shame
I seem to have lost my way

You said to hold on
I inferred a long wait
I held on beyond reason
You perceived procrastination
At last I let go
Your promise an empty echo

The flock has flown as I clutched to belief
Now and alone it was just a dream
Having lost all direction I seek true reflection
But it's only an image
Distorted misperception

It's dangerous to fly ahead of the clan
Knock yourself out and have nowhere to land
Can't keep formation without knowing the plan
Fly into closed windows of someone else's house
Or else follow blindly lost in the crowd

The bird flies south for the winter
Seeking a longer day
Shuts out the cold for the warmth and pleasure
Of its own instinctive way

*

62.

Sometimes I feel a storm inside
Sometimes I feel my heart's capsized
And I am left adrift

For all the roles I've played in life
Of al_ those that I've left behind
I think I'm happiest

A costume stained and torn apart
A body aging and worn out
A soul at peace is best

*

63.

Impatience
Simple fear
Disturbance
Obstruction of the flow of harmony

A worry
Of something that probably doesn't exist
Won't happen
Unless we want it badly enough

Anxiety
Oblivious to reality
Burning out the nervous system
Impeding sensibility

Anger
Panic
Destruction of immunity
Relax

*

64.

Fear is awareness of weakness
Courage is perception of strength
Awareness arrives on the plane of thought
We are what we think

And everybody knows this
Though we commonly discard it
To ingest television images
We are not independent

But rather interdependent
Upon each other's views
We've evolved the urge to merge our minds
On common ground if we choose

But this is a lengthy process
Worthy of a lifetime
To actually put into practice
Ideas of so many minds

And as each generation
Follows the one before
We pick up our elders' sweet revelations
Discarded as burdensome chores

*

65.

The biggest bend in the road
And those who didn't go back
Either turned or went on ahead

I'm camped out by that road
With nowhere safe to go
No one with whom to share the quest
There's just no point anymore
When the point was to interact
And I'm left alone instead

When the infinite is in each soul
Most may a missing piece forego
Renewing from the rest

And what I suffer none will know
Or see me standing by the road
A thoroughfare indifference

Perishable in the silence
Of mislaid hope and innocence
Invisible and unknown

For if the waves don't intersect
There is no image to project
And I've nowhere to go

*

66.

Relax and be where you will
So many concerns are borrowed
We owe it to ourselves once in a while
To throw everybody else's world out the window
And live in our own for a while

Relaxing is restitution
For all the senseless worries
That seemed like a good idea at the time

It's necessary to lay quiet
To be still, to rest
And refresh everything
Through dreams

*

67.

Indigestion
Swallowing thoughts not understood
Unable to put them to use

Fast
Rest
Digest

Assimilate
What has been heard
And learn

*

68.

You can know what you cannot know by other's
standards
And sometimes you can shut your eyes and ears
Only to have the outside well up inside
Through dreams

Dreams are the lights of our inner minds
That truly are ourselves
And sometimes we feel what we cannot touch

We hold hands only to let go again
Sometimes we are many people in dreams
And what we do while awake to each other
We really do to ourselves

*

69.

If time has eluded you
Stop and find it
You have to dig up emotions
To rebuild after time is disrupted

*

70.

Never say you understand
It lets the others know
Your feelings are a doormat
They'll wipe their feet and go

Forgiveness ends a friendship
Transgresses further on
All you have been taught was good
Is what you have done wrong

Then death will come and claim us
And leave this unresolved
All because of empathy
You chose to trample on

*

71.

Greatness is discrimination
That forgives
Fault finding is theft of dignity

It buries the victim
In a shroud of secrecy
Unconditional acceptance
Is a gift of great esteem

It takes a lot of energy
To hear and understand
Or even just accept

It takes a lot of empathy
To feel and comprehend
Or simply just accept

Listening takes a lot of strength
And lots of energy
One must step outside oneself
To listen actively

And that means letting go the need
To be the centerpiece
Listening lets the other hear
The voice of empathy

*

72.

Pride begins when respect dims
For the vision of vastness greater souls see
Humility is the open door
Through which flows gentle mercy

Death begins when darkness creeps in
And thought turns away from the light
And when the body's end is reached
One has a chance to reawaken from sleep

The escape into breathlessness
To float through the iridescent mist of timelessness
To the vibration underlying creation
And know

We are the colors of the rainbow
When we stop laughing
We start growing old

*

45

73.

We climb through the web
Trying not to get tangled
Remembering where we come from
And how we got here

The answers outside disintegrate
When put to the test of reality
The answers within help us calibrate
Just where it is we've come to be

*

74.

I can accept cause and effect
But only an abusive God would test
Her own children

It's a man-made concept
Of which God has been convicted
On circumstantial evidence

Until we learn to forgive
God's not the prosecutor
But the defendant

*

75.

The river springs forth from the boundary
Between inside and out
And flows forth from the vulnerable depths
Of feeling, hope and doubt

Into the vastness of mass creation
To wash clean the impurities of fear
Vision blurred by an eye bruised
By years of tears

And constantly the tide flows in
And out
In the crashing roar of breaking waves
See the dream of nights and days

Merge into the world as we know it
That can only be seen by acting in it
The vastness of ocean all around us
If we could only see it

*

76.

Mysterious lesson plan
Hidden from me
In a brief life span

It simplifies
Then complicates
Til I realize
All has been a mistake

We are creatures of a simple race
Expanded egos and pretty faces
It's easier to love an idiot
Than a destructive genius

*

47

77.

Overcrowded prisons
Traps we have set for ourselves
So many trapped in a mindless disposal

It is us we fear
We cannot control confusion
So we want to confine the world

Natural spontaneity
Deteriorates into impulse
And we are ashamed

Some say leniency
Some say punishment
I say let us not judge

*

78.

There is a place in all of us
Deep and dark
Afraid to touch
Where what's so right horrifies
What's so bright blindly defies
Common sense

The little things that we do best
The pieces that fit everyday life
Lie bereft of greatness
Of extremes

Cause when we wander to the edge
We tilt the balance
And awaken that darkness
Deep in all of us
Just when you think
You've done something great
Someone great comes along and tells you
To learn how to love

*

79.

I'm not who I once thought I was
I've misinterpreted myself
It was just a mask to hide the loss
Of my real face on the shelf

The pain required a cover up
The emptiness of a hollow shell
Echoing harshly over again
Guilt clapper of the silver bell

But an empty heart has no reliable beat
No rhythm on which to count
The incomplete must be reconstructed
After the plague of doubt

Approval and esteem
Captivate my thoughts
Bestowed only in dreams
While untold time is lost

Fair angel flying through the world
Take note of one in fear
Who desperately craving affection
Wants you to greet me here

A lifetime of feeling excluded
A nighttime of being left out
Has left me living a lonely illusion
Sunshine obscured by clouds

Fair spirit passing through my space
Grace me with a smile
Release the fear that clouds my face
And stay with me a while

*

80.

Time distorts our feelings and movements
As we try to sing in different rhythms
We hear what we listen for
And see what we want to see

But there are conflicts with the currents
That surround and sway us
On the battleground of converging fronts
Fighting for control of you and me

If you're overwhelmed
Bend
And if you're pushed
Fall free

*

81.

All is one
The hand of God reaches down
Its fingers into bodies of matter
All one body of spirit
Extended into each of us
Beings touched
By the hand of God

Boundaries blur
Til I can't tell who is myself
Living the ultimate expression
Of society's spiritual pathology
Reaching down
Into my cells

We have merged
And met deep in the current
Of the river that flows through us all
And in denial
Failed to recognize our cells

*

82.

Truth creeps in to spill its seeds
It's a sword in the side of human
For the lies we believe and the lies we tend
Lie waiting to self-destruct when
The simplicity we strive to escape
Stares back in the form of a dying face

*

83.

Form is important
It manifests spirit
Both ever changing

Can you hear it
The voice of your dream
Telling you the way of change

It is momentum
It is the moment
It is the choices you make

As emotion rises
Spins ever faster
It crosses the boundaries we've made

Between each other
To join together
In the dance of the ages

*

84.

Everyone's leaving town
A disappearing drone of a plane
Footsteps fading in the distance
Car motors starting away
A whole town of people going away

The time is mass confusion
In the midst of massive emotion
Who can comprehend the madness of a nation
While it still lives?

Love yet ungiven
Cries for understanding
Among the masses

The time is always passing
We're all wearing down
Eyesight fades
Steps stumble and fall
The sounds around us fade away

Hope twinkles in the eye
That recognizes beauty
And smiles

*

85.

Dream is not hallucination
As it seems to some
But the door to reality
Of all that's been done

The heart is the key
To open the eyes
To see where we've been
Hiding in time

*

86.

Raw emotion is unpleasant
Refined and processed is unnatural
But easier to digest

If only we could go back in time
If only we always had a chance
To edit our lives

Instead we can only
Observe ourselves closely
And choose carefully

Patient discretion
Is the ultimate diploma
From life's lesson

*

87.

Why so lonely?
How long in the womb
To heal the sorrow
Of internal wounds

I think I knew
And then I'm lost
In a social whirlwind
Of muted myth

Isolated
Abandoned
Like a dream walker
Grasping the wind

How much longer?
What to know?
How lies tomorrow
Time the unknown

Dreams and life shared
But left unspoken
To piece together
As self unbroken

*

88.

Anger is the willingness
To admit the need for change
It is only destructive
When chained

I used to think it an illness
An irritation burning inside
Until it hurt so bad I broke
And cried

Now I know its benefits
Thunder clears the air
You only get angry when
You care

*

89.

Competence is an issue frequently overlooked
By consumer mentalities
That don't care what they have to do
To satisfy their greed

There are no limits to freedom of personal expression
Except expressed by oneself
The essence of beauty has many dimensions
Fragrance smells of heaven and hell

Competence is a flower blooming in silence
For those that like themselves
Nature has never stopped producing
For itself

Those tangled in intricate book-learned knowledge
Those caught in mind-baffling games of power
Should notice the obvious simplicity
Of flowers

*

90.

Wrapped up in his own world inside his head
He comes out to visit less and less
The world becomes empty when you don't listen

When you don't let new thoughts in
The old ones echo over again
And grow old

*

91.

When we're searching for the answers
And trying to understand
We're looking for an audience
Someone to give us a hand

Nature is mostly accidents
Acceptance understands
Nature expresses the infinite
Perceived by appreciative humans

Society superimposes its rules
With no instruction but façade
A social club massage of egos
That stops spontaneous love

The game didn't come with instructions
The elitists took them out of the box
And hid them away for a select privileged few
Who join the club of rules

Purists afraid of accidents
Of Nature's continuous pun
Loneliness only wanted an audience
All that's needed is spontaneous fun

We're children locked away in a room
Making up artificial rules
Because no one showed us the doors and windows
Or gave us the keys or tools

The elitists locked them up somewhere
And didn't want to share
All I wanted to do was get out
And get a breath of fresh air

I had to pretend to play the game
To find out how it's done
I learned it from Nature's accidents
The goal is appreciation

Door openers are persecuted by churches
Exclusivity protects their inhibitions
From exposure to threatening revelations
Nature's not a social club

Deep down in the river of life
We merge together as one
Simplicity doesn't alienate
The way aristocracy does

Religion hides the key to the soul
Perception's the key that opens the door
But if the price of admission is alienation
I don't want to play anymore

*

92.

I sit back in the comfort of my warm bed
And look out my window for answers
It's easy to find confusion in my head
There are lots of contradictions in my life

Life
It is mine
I used to wonder where I would live
Then I realized I am alive

*

93.

My mother was born in Caruthersville
In her youth she moved away
So the river wouldn't carry her away
Small town stayed with her all her life
Open book raging like the river
Under Twain's darker shadow
River of feelings damned by dislikes
Instead of being free to flow

*

94.

Like a rose when full
Is incomprehensible
To a linear mind
True feeling reaches deep enough
To touch the heart
And imprint itself in the brain's memory cells
To not be erased with time

The reservoir of hidden genius
Stranded on an island in a sea of thought
Where emotion escapes logic
And the heart defies the mind
When the senses are exhausted from working overtime
Sleep unlocks the door to dream
And feeling

Looking out at the world
Self-consciousness destroys consciousness
Feeling shatters fact
Until you step outside yourself
And look in
Nothing has to fall back into place
Everything is as it is

*

95.

Be still and wait
Wait for me to light the torch myself
Everyone makes their own light

Flickering through the prism
Light from the artist's brush splatters
As it enters time and matter

Understanding, soul and universe
Masked in the simplicity of primary colors
Painted by the dreaming artist

*

96.

I feel the distance between us when we speak
Disappear when we touch
Your words fall like rocks on the cavern floor
Mine echo to be swallowed by the darkness
And your breathing is almost still
But I am still and can listen
To the labors of your chest
The rustling bat wing beyond
The swallow bidding from the mouth
Of the cave we lie lost in
Which way will you go?

*

97.

Throw yourself into the ocean
And feel the rhythms in the current
Complicated, intricate
The basis of life

If you don't adjust to those rhythms
Bombarding your body and your soul
You'll sink and fight and drown

Just mingle into them and float
Float, drift, blend
And you'll wonder if this knows
Anything of time
And soon you find you know far more
By just being

Join the current and blend
A grain of sand in the ocean
Floating through ripples from distant lands
Colliding with waves in rhythmic convergence
You learn just to be there
Is to live

*

98.

Nothing I say is new
It's all been said before
I've lots of catching up to do
I've been this way before

There is light ahead
We can go safely around the bend
Knowing there is no dead end

*

99.

Why is it so hard to love
Those that don't love themselves?
Love is blocked by condemnation
We must forgive ourself

Judging manifests a barrier
That really isn't there
Implies a crime that didn't happen
Presumes insight in the unaware

The child isn't taught by example to love
The child doesn't see, doesn't feel that it's loved
Doesn't believe it can be loved
Isn't free to be part of anyone

Where does it all end?
Someone wakes up starved for affection
Hungry for love, craving attention
And cries

Somewhere inside
The universal parent of existence
Responds

*

100.

I fumble clumsily through the days
And nights of peopled menageries
Trying to cling to something substantial
And mend my broken dreams

Ice reclaims what was living
To let misdirection freeze in deep sleep
Those far from reality lose animation
Unless they touch their feelings again

Learn to accept what is given
Silence the mind and hear the heart
Cry
And dream again

*

101.

I wonder if I'm losing my grip on youth
That a stranger seems foreign to me now
Instead of a potential friend

So many alienations with which to contend
Isolated by walls, lack of vision and fear
Surely I must be dreaming this nightmare

A deaf world whose only ears are dead trees
Paper—my silent audience
Never answers me

*

102.

Storms erase the past
So we can forgive and forget
But there comes a time when we have to remember
And admit

Lost in the night in a city of walls
Lights sparkle in a pavement puddle
And gyrate to the drumming of pounding feet
Hurrying to be somewhere else

Glimmering places within dreary caves
That echoes flow around
Where tears and fears of years have condensed
Into shimmering forms

There is a pattern that continues through time
Within the dark recesses of the mind
And all we have to do to find it
Is remember

*

103.

Words so intimate with the mind
Describe the physical as differences
Light is the force that builds living cells
The body is an echo of thought

Revealing in the eyes the way we see ourselves
The sky is there but I cannot hold it
The barrier is the emptiness
Of thought

Our shadows have led us out of the dark
Distances are measured in words
Listen to the echoes of thoughts
To feel the feelings of earth

Take the pieces of your broken glass heart
And make them a wind chime
A song of joy

Witness the vision of a small blossom
Hidden amidst tall grass
Intricate and delicately bright as day
Complete and true in every way

A sunbeam journeys so far from home
To warm a tiny blade of grass
That it has never known

Be as the firelight that warms the cold
As a sunbeam that journeys
So far from home

Un rayo viaja lejos de sol
Para calentar la hierba
Nunca ha conocido

*

104.

Death arrives suddenly in a dream
Stalks the dark night veiled and sinister
The body freezes cold in terror
Of the unexpected unknown horror
Face it
It's what you've been waiting for

*

105.

Light enters through the door of simplicity
Perception replaces boundaries
The dreamer projects this hologram
Throughout eternity

*

106.

Straight edged plateaus
Expressed in flowing line
That leads far away
Into Colorado snows
Forming a background
For the rounded swells
Of ravine etched earth

Treasure boxes of splotches of color
And patches of sand
Where the shadow of a cloud is impressed
A splendid sun makes love to a silent land
As my impassioned eye indulges
In desert tenderness

*

107.

Enter a flower upon a stage
A spaceship on a voyage
Echo the time in a mirror of rhyme

I am a butterfly lost in the stars
Frightened and crazy and bold
Loved and yet so much alone

Enter a pebble upon a beach
A voice beyond your reach
Remember the smile that would not speak

I have a right to share your world
If I can touch your soul
Love so strange but well known

Enter a willow in a storm
A bed sheet stained and torn
Enter a butterfly in flight

A comet in the night
Capture the moment by touching form
And soar into the light

*

108.

Suddenly vanquished from the winds
Isolated in the tornado's eye
Like a passage out of context
Instantaneously disincarnate
Lost on the border of the winds

Before moving on you have seen a cloud
Pass from the atmosphere to the unseen
And you gave it no thought
Now you try to recall where you've seen this before
But you cannot

*

109.

A creature as capable of love as human
Must have a vaster home than this
Must hold the universe in her hand
If she would only realize it

Earth is small
Within the universe
This traveler with direction
A place of gentle spirit

Here a quiet miracle
Where spirit has settled
Some pass on
Without being aware

A nomad in space
Fortressed against nothing
Charged yet uncaring against all extremes
So should I dare to be

*

110.

In a destitute time the Earth stood still
Unprepared for what was to come
And silently she held all breath
As you opened your eyes and nestled in her arms
And kindled in your mother warm
Preservation of feeling and expression
Spoken in the wind and the ocean's tides
Written in the stones of the mountainsides
And cradled in her heart
The thought of love will never die
But live in the treasure of the flower that you are

*

111.

The page of color turns
Awakens an inner urge
That churns the tangible
And purges interdimensional

I no longer find you here
There was a star in the sky
I saw only at night
And only for half the year

The newness of absolute touch
Opening all directions
Unfolding sepal and stamen
With innocent intentions

For inspiration stillness
For duty we rationalize
For beauty all is willing
For beauty all is kind

The rain will come again
Wash away the dirt again
Sparkle in the sun again
The sun will shine again

*

112.

Reality is the color
When the flower
Is occupied with fragrance

*

113.

Emotional swells dismember my thoughts
That fall fadingly like shooting stars
Across the ceiling of my world
To eternal horizons

*

114.

Our atoms are a molecule
In the universe of time
Horizon meets horizon now
Nowhere to hide

Somewhere in a spectrum of worlds
That you share with me
Your atoms merge with thoughts of mine
And manifest reflectively

Adrift in a biological sea
I marvel at the habits we bring into being
To appease our insecurity
And occupy our freedom

In a vast expanse of space and mind
Thought flies out to sea
And like distant lights across the night
Thoughts reach back to me

*

115.

Could the sun allow only one beam come to Earth?
Just one arm of light from the sky?
Could I ever love just you alone?
Could the sun light one leaf and let all others die?

*

116.

How fragile is the individual dream
I will not shatter what you see
Make me a door that's open
A clear path past all the worlds
That lie between you and me

*

117.

Lightning down below
Lines of playful light
Life is stirring in the planet womb
The butterfly still sleeps inside its warm cocoon
The time to fly is coming soon

Windows of time
That need not exist anymore
The windows have been opened
And all has come to turn
Now I have stepped into your world
Above the glow of Saturn

Gateways defined
That need not exist anymore
The gates have closed behind us
Past and future in turn
Meet me for the journey home
Inside the rings of Saturn

Memories of blue
Swirling ocean mist
Life awakens in an abandoned crib
The butterfly now resting at its end
The breath of life drifts on the wind

Echoes of minds
No longer one anymore
Our signs have come together
Stars and firelight burn
Share with me the mystic's lore
Inside the rings of Saturn

*

118.

Who thinks they are the first to speak intelligently
Who has the insight to claim philosophy
When the winged have been singing
Throughout eternity

Such a noise mankind is making
Such self-indulgence in shaking and rumbling
Echoes of an earthquake crumbling a mountain
Because its rocks could not sleep together

*

119.

Like looking for your hat
When it's on your head
Like looking for your eyeglasses
Sitting on your nose
Chasing rainbows

*

120.

A lullaby lows as I lie down
A nightingale—an owl
That softly howls

Frozen wind brings cold and pain
Cruel wind in twisters and hurricanes
Soft breeze, harsh wind, living breath

All the same

*

121.

Nestled in the armpits of purple peaks
Evergreens shaped like tipis
Wear arrow tips of forest green

Miles and miles within eyesight
Etchings of agaves
X'd deeply in ravines
In between jagged rock formations
Catch the eye on yellow flower patches
Opening the door of a dream

For only in dreams one finds misplaced menageries
Such as these
Evergreens and tumbleweeds
Dinosaur bones and adobe

Crows and craters and beachless white sands
Roadrunners and lava domes
Hot air balloons ascending in mass
Till you awake and are gone

*

122.

A present came to me in my dreams
A star with a ribbon on it
Trust given in vulnerability
Force beyond creation

Of that which creates
Which is itself
Beyond time and space
All-flexible

Fixed in ultimate transition
The dream of freedom to dream
It is the idea of ourselves we must let go of
To trust creation

*

123.

I walked along a dirt path
Past fields being dug up for parks
The young pines nearly had grown into woods
That were not there when I was young
Past the fields in the woods the spring had come
And I found the old path I used to walk down
When I was young

The trees hid me from the plows in the fields
And gave my eyes shade from the sun
In solitude their branches were full
Of animation and song
Then off to my left a new path had been worn
By feet the size of mine when I was young
So I followed it deep into woods I had not known
When I was young

And it wove around among the trees
And led to a small clearing
In its midst an old pine crucified
By small hands with hammer and nails
An old pine silent and willing
Not asking for comfort from me
I stayed a while touching the texture of its bark
And found a smile in me

So I followed the path back
To another old tree I had known when I was young
And there we stood alone
But the path beside it was wider now
And where it used to stop traveled on
And I wondered how long this sweet gum still had
Knowing soon it would be cut down by the path
And asked how it felt to be part of the land
As starry leaves whispered an epitaph:

God's wife is the Earth
All life is their son
Their spirit is in us
Their spirit is love

*

124.

We're all ash
Those who haven't been through the fire yet
Are in a state of hesitation
But only those who don't hesitate
Will get anything done

It's what the tree produced before it was cut down
That amounts to any good
And if it was already dead and dried
Goes up like a puff of nonexistent wood

Sap that lingers prolongs consciousness
Long enough to gain awareness
That lingers in the ash

I am ash
I have felt the fire
I could perform all the good in the world now
None of which could amount to the magnitude
Of what I might have done before

*

125.

Wings of light on solar winds
Energy and particles of all that I've been
Being the lamp that lights the path
I am all the love I have given

Light burst forth from seven suns
Like an explosion of all I've become
A supernova of realization
I've chosen who I am

*

126.

We've all been stung
By each other's troubles
In spite of what we've not done

There's sense in the nonsense
If group interference
Is taken into account

You're not a devil
You're not a star
You always belong where you are

*

127.

The flight of the sparrow
Has crossed the ocean of dreams
Across blue skies and fields of stars
By patience the sparrow is free

Entering another dimension
Like being born under a different sun
All around is spinning
All that is living is love
Diving deeply within
Tearing away until pain is gone
The universe is shimmering
In an internal chasm of love

The ocean between us is parted
Dreams waking in the still of night
The curtain between us unveiled
By the sparrow's timeless flight

*

128.

Once upon a time
The world was well defined
Now what was real
Is not so real
And all around is sky

This wasn't supposed to happen
In the way the world once was
I didn't know this could happen
Wings unfurling from my heart

Floating, falling, flying
Feelings flickering like stars
Out there your world is very real
From here so very far

When we're standing on the ground
No words will say to you
We kissed out there among the stars
And I know it's you

*

129.

Global upheaval
Lives uprooted
A planet in revolution
When has it not been so?

Who are we?
Racing frantically
Desperate for survival
Feelings are trampled

Some come forward
To lead the way
Their way
But each must find their own

Don't mistake the flame that lights the way
For the ultimate destination

*

130.

Daisies are the smiles of the gods
And the flattery of gardens
To attract butterflies
To bed with them

*

131.

I believe in dream shine
The echo of your heart
Looking across the galaxy
We change the world with what we see
We have held creation in our love

*

132.

I see your smile in the smiles of others
And in the sunshine of the day
I send my smile to you in moonlight
And listen to echoes when you're away

But I hear your whisper of breath in my ear
And know deep inside you are touching me
Like the magic of a rainbow between sky and earth
Your spirit is holding hands with me

*

133.

Stars are bright
But planets have substance
The duality of what we think is real

Stars shine
But clouds that shield them
Wield the mystery of life

Rain gives birth
But tears are feelings
That fall from the darkest stars of night

Eyes see
But closed dream
And understand

*

134.

We project illusions of external limits
Nature has no insurmountable walls
Cliffs and mountains can be risen above
Or explored
Like a mountain your roots run deep
But you are not as hard as you think
A gentle breeze—a river of tears
Can wear you down

Deep in the caves of your depths
It would crush me if you were to collapse
Your stillness protects me
My will is your inner support

And our separateness is our illusion
Myth is the reality of the human condition
As your thought echoes in my heart
We exist together

*

135.

I feel like it was yesterday
You came into my heart
Now all the pain has burned away
The clouds begin to part
And sunlight shines upon the day
You came into my heart

Up the chimney Santa goes
Above the darkness we have flown
Together with one soul
From decay the flower grows
Gentle blossoms will unfold
Wherever you may go

I know it was just yesterday
You tore my soul apart
But the pain has burned away
And now you've lit the dark
And sunlight shines upon the day
You came into my heart

Up from the ashes Phoenix rose
Above the smoke clouds we have flown
And bright light shines upon the day
You became my home

*

136.

Can't look at the sun and see
But look and see what the sun sees
Stare at the sun and it will blind
The way to see is to be the light

*

137.

The words you whisper
Are like the wind
Sad but beautiful
And like the wind
I cannot hold you
Like the wind
Your shadow shows you

Your lullaby
Is like the rain
Gentle and renewing
But like the rain
The river runs down
A strand of lonely tears
Flows down my face

Pain into compassion grows
And breaks the shell that once confined
Pain that cannot be contained
The shell surrenders freely
Opens wide
A river of pearls
Flows from my eyes

*

138.

Early morning humidity
The Earth is crying for something
That never came to be

Once there was kindness
Once tenderness
But something tilted the balance

Something hid the plan
And now we search for buried treasure
When we hold all in our hand

                              *

139.

Vivid dreams are hard to separate
From waking life
And why not?
They're easier to understand

Vivid faces I know I haven't met
But when they look familiar I know I will
The flow of time is temporarily suspended
What I think I know is interrupted

While awake our senses are safe
Particles brushed by waves
Sheltered from the intensity of light
By an umbrella we call the other side

The atmosphere of creation
Laced with protective striations
Like tender clouds with gentle rains
That flow as quietly as grasses' dew

Angels' hair gently caresses you
And touches you in dreams

And in a moment's meditation
You lose yourself in concentration
Beyond your senses' scope
The key to wisdom overheard

The meaning of life in a murmured word
Remembered as a mystery whispered
All things of matter unite themselves
In the spirit of the universe

*

140.

Dancing in dreams
Above the city
Where a flower grows
On a mountain in the stars
The seed is ours

In the stillness
In the silent sky
Eternity
In an ocean of stars

Love is a garden of stars
And the seed is ours

*

141.

Faces clouded and dark inside
Faces like moons reflecting sunlight
People often like to hide
In the group with which they identify

In some eyes I see no sunshine
Nor darkened clouds of doubt
But the emptiness of fear
Hollow space with day and night left out

*

142.

From where you stand
I travel in circles
It seems we have crossed paths

From where she sits
I weave back and forth
It seems we have crossed swords
But I look down and see
How far I've risen
We appear as separate
In limited dimension

Though it isn't obvious
To our near-sighted vision
Paths travel at once
In multiple directions

*

143.

The change in the tide isn't sudden
The seasons don't just come and go
They return
And no wind ever starts up instantly
That wasn't there before
As the lake pours into the ocean
And yesterday into today
You have gradually crept into my heart
And influenced all of my ways

*

144.

Your eyes are preoccupied
Shining stars
But it's the clouds of mystery
That fall in tears upon me

Elusive, distant, invisible
All behind your eyes
The soul's revelation lies submerged
Behind your clouded eyes

*

145.

The rain is loud of splash and drip
A wailing moan cries from the wind
Snowflakes are silent

*

146.

I'm the hopeless optimist
Finding the sun in the dark
Singing to no one but the stars
You heard my song one night

I tried to sing my heart to you
All the beauty and pain
I tried so hard to sign my name
Where do words go in dreams?

I am your lover in the unknown
Outwardly inverted inside
Repressed rejection exploding
Into sparkling lights

Under the moon our thoughts echo back
Love gives light to the day
Touch me again—the particles spin
And together become a wave

*

147.

⁀Moonlight in your eyes
Sounds of starlight penetrate
The darkness of night sky

Echoes in my dreams
Whisper from around the world
Of what we seem to be
Feel the light that will not dim
In your sight my love
Pick the flower that will not wilt
In your hand my love
In your hand

Sunbeam from my heart
Why it is I do not know
Or how this love could start

Heed the rising moon
Feelings shared in passion's flight
Sunbeam comes to you

Taste the flower the rain has filled
With our tears my love
Pick the flower that will not wilt
In your heart my love
In your heart

*

95

148.

Life is made of dreams and hopes
And you're in all of mine
And music gives the soul a joy
That nowhere else you'd find

Once your song had touched my heart
The wings of love took flight
And in your arms I've seen the world
From heaven's lofty heights

In the darkness of my fears
I hear your gentle mind
Calling me beyond my fears
To once upon a time

Tomorrow is your choice, my love
I leave you to decide
But know because I love you
Heaven's always by your side

If you would only love me
The stars could shine tonight
And flowers color of the sun
Would blossom in your sight

The love I have to share with you
Is the flower of my life
And if you would only love me
The stars would shine tonight

*

149.

All I have is the fate to wait
And stumble in eternity
And the faith to wait
Until heaven comes to me
And turns my face to the sun
If I walk away alone
But I still know how to care
I may always be lonely
But I won't condone despair

*

150.

Some people crush flowers for medicine
A weed is a flower you have no use for
You see what you want to see
A cup filled with love was broken
And the pieces thrown away
A weed mowed down with the grass
Who can say who hurt more?
Some people crush flowers for medicine

*

151.

Identity is hard to define
When too many others get in the way
You have to decide
Yourself

*

152.

On the edge of a spinning disc
The realm of stars descends
Upon the spinning Earth
Far beyond the galaxy
The flower of the universe

Fly away little seed
I send you on your way little seed
Fly up to the mountain
Like lost galaxies in flight
Little flowers flying kites
Fly away little seed
Into night light

On the edge of a spinning disc
Flip the coin—which side is me?
In the arms of the galaxy
Comforted by harmony
Light is latent melody

Fly away little note
I send you on your way little note
Fly far beyond all sound
Like lost electrons all around
The chorus sounds cling to your core
Fly away little note
And bring back more

Levitation accelerates
Traversing the octaves
Halve the wave in a leap of faith
Communicate harmonics
Tuned to reality

Fly away my soul
I send you on your way my soul
Fly far beyond all breath
Like lost children found in death
The spirit flower blossoms forth
Fly away my soul
And bring back more

*

153.

We focus on differences
To distinguish between us
We constantly choose
Where to focus our sight
For all the different types of lamps
There's just one light

*

154.

So many rivers
Supply a continent
Trillions of grains of sand and dirt
Condensed into a planet

I don't think I could change the world
I'd rather leave it alone
I've learned to be patient
I've nowhere else to go

*

155.

Being particular is my defense
Against desperation
For fear of rejection
I'd accept anyone who'd have me
And end up in the dregs of society
With others lacking self-esteem
Like me

And that's where I learned we're all the same
And that's where I found how to play the game
How to be what you want to be
Instead of what you've been taught to be
It's very important what you believe
Because it always comes true

So many good people being told they're no good
By churches believing in evil
And all is pain until you've understood
Your own good is what you will
If you will be good

Believe you are nothing and you will have nothing
You will have no values
Nothing will have meaning
Blaming society for your misery
Till it punishes you for being angry
What you believe is what you prove

I made the choice to choose my beliefs
Against the protests of those around me
I insisted I deserved the best
I challenged their belief in failure
Churches failed
But God passed the test

Being particular I learned to accept
In disbelief I found hard fact
There's a way for everyone
If you will
Be blessed

*

156.

Sounding cheerful and always hopeful
The vastness of sky is for the birds
And when I listen I know full well
Their wisdom exceeds my words

The mountain kisses the sky
As I watch safely below
Tucked in a blanket of evergreens

No army can conquer this mountain inside me
No one can bring me to my knees
No evil can cast me into dungeons of darkness
As long as there are places like these

I've changed directions several times
Changed careers, changed my mind
Every path just leads within
Now silence claims the dim outside
But for a feather in the wind

No devil can darken this heaven inside me
No sadness can silence your endless tune
No betrayal can falter the wisdom of friendship
Having known a little bird like you

*

157.

Simplicity draws back the curtains
Rainbow peeks through window prism
As I center in a world of time
On the receiving end of light

As soon as light is sought
The shadow speaks its demanding heart
And I cannot tell its voice apart
From myself

Softness can be might
The mind should follow the heart
With all the stars that shine
There needn't be a dark

*

158.

Arte de Dios
Realeza en todos
Infinito cactos alcanzan por el cielo
Zanjas y mesas a rayas en el desierto
Opaco y cerca el cañón grande
Natural y piedra preciosa árboles
Arte grandioso

Art by God
Royalty in all that stands
Infinite cactus arms reach for the sky
Zebra stripes dyed exotic colors stretch across the land
Opening into a sculpted chasm
Notched into vast breathtaking expanse
And antelopes that pose for pictures if you ask

God painted the earth
And sculpted the trees
Into precious gems
For his bride to be

*

159.

I'll tell you the truth
Before I lose my mind
Loving is not wrong
And lying is not right
I'm a star who's lost her way
A comet lost in time

Why I've come here
Is hard to know
To move so fast
In a world so slow

Love's the momentum
A force not defined
By gravity illusions
Directions or time

In a sky where kindness grows
The secrets of the soul
Are shadowed in mystery
To shatter the ego
And lose the false identity
That masks the face of love

A twin within duality
But what am I searching for?
To stand upon the threshold
Where love is ever more

An arrow struck me
When I found my wings
The archer has held me
In my dreams

His night holds my day
Severed this bird would lose her wings
And song
And fade away

*

160.

Clouds of doubt
Forces of thought
Turning in every direction
Looking for a way out

Sword drawn
Upturned and piercing
Clouds without cutting
Or dispersing

Particle spinning
Increasing momentum
Breaks the uncertainty barrier
To peace

Beyond the stars
There is no measure
Beyond the dream
There is ever peace

Somewhere
Before the beginning
After disturbance
Returning

*

105

161.

Light the fire
Warm the room
Melt the snow

Drink the water
Wash your hands
Of the snow

Stomp the beauty
Clump the mass
Mash the snow

Don your coat
Step outside
Watch the snow

*

162.

Another change in another year
Another bend in an old branch
Like a candy stick worn down to a point
The edges of life blend together

I watch a leaf dance toward my head
The sky bends over and tucks the heather into bed
And all is well

*

163.

A flower is a priceless work of love
And a perfect work of art
A metaphysical masterpiece
Complete with an angel's heart
Flowers spring back in spite of all
Such power the little things hold
That in all the wilderness humans create
They continue to grow

Expression of life past and future
Toil's bridge of crowning glory
Extends perfection in magnificent gems
On the stems of all in its garden

Flower is the highest form of art
Color and smell of sensuous lure
God without body
Could never be as pure

*

164.

Forgive what I do not know
Over the centuries
Letters in the silence flow
The gap of time is closing in
Handle me gently
So soon again our paths have crossed
Swords drawn in exchanged thoughts
Memory keys unlocked
The door between beings opening wide
It's just a matter of time

*

165.

The strongest emotions evoke the rhythm
Sensitivity strikes the rhyme
Tunnel vision searches for the light
As polarity masks the other side

It's easy to share good feelings with friends
But anger is a dangerous expression
So the feelings pour onto the page
Where the only harm is freedom

*

166.

Nothing old, nothing new
Just a lot of nerve
Motive guides our little wills
To the purpose we serve

We can have what we want if we will
If we ration hopes and dreams
And rationalize ideal

Will writes destiny
It's all probability
Awesome idea
Choose what to be

But carefully
For what effect follows
To interject reality

Imagination turns the wheel
There is but one stipulation
We must redefine what is real

*

167.

The dawn of a day
On a world at peace
I picture it quiet
And void of people

I don't know where to start again
Because I know I'll get hurt again
It's not the fear but the shame
Of rejection

Temperatures are rising
But the world is bitter cold
I haven't the strength to call the bid
So I guess I'll just have to fold

But presents appear in strange places
Acceptance abides in the heart
Gifts are where we find them
I'm trying to find a fresh start

Clever words and casual rhyme
Phrases that can turn on a dime
Reveal the soreness and the pain
Of the sublime

I've been sitting on the fence
While surrounded by extremes
I'm not here to be convinced
I just want to caress the breeze

*

168.

Rest from struggle to start again
Is the universal goal of human
In good will is kindly strength

Throw off the anxious nervousness
By calmly facing its cause
Remember the source of all
Let it flow

Intimacy—that vulnerable tenderness
Is sensitivity at its finest
Without it I am senseless

Run from the voice of dread inside
Fight the habit to fault find
And disagree with all that's disagreeable
Serenity is sensitively sensible

Relax and let the world unfold
Indulging the universal show
Of the moment

*

169.

The air is salty and chilled
The sand is moist and cold
And the clouds look back at my naked existence
As if I was a story they told
Along their endless trek tonight

And I ask a broken seashell
How I came to be here this time
A shell that belongs in the homeless waters
Drifting in the wandering tide
Ejected from the revolving sea
To bury itself in the sand
And contemplate the beach

*

170.

Global warming is a myth
This world is glaciating
Communication shutting down
From lack of feeling

People are too busy
To answer the phone and talk
Instead you're expected to record your message
And get lost

Civilization is isolation
We are truly free
From attachment to each other
Separate and lonely

It's all part of a bigger plan
To make us realize
How cut off we are from our higher self
So we will reunite

*

171.

It would all be over in a flash
I knew I couldn't understand
Until I would look back

And nothing is as it seems
Life more vivid than dreams
You look back free

From the pain of duality
Stupidity of condemnation
Hypocrisy of misunderstanding

You know you're right
And then the lightning strikes

*

172.

Revenge is an empty shell
That has lost its pearl to the diver thief
Anger has robbed the soul blind
It makes its stand upon the beach

But cannot defy the tide
That will grind it into sand
It dared to stand upon
In ignorance

*

173.

The days are laid out ahead of us
Nights and stars will always fall
And people progress through all
The wars and hurricanes and holocausts
The sieges, debris and isolation
Most continue to love

Some go through a wedding without making a marriage
Become a parent without learning patience
To be born human
And curse others for mistakes
I could just as well blame the whole human race
For my situation

There is no measure for love
It doesn't matter how empty one is
All that matters is if you love him
That's all anyone is
We might think we're important
But we'd rather just be loved

*

174.

Foolish to issue ultimatums
Leading ultimately to destruction
There is always another way

*

175.

Hate eventually destroys itself
Prejudice consumes its own heart
Knowledge vanquishes ignorance
As light annihilates dark

I met you in a new world
Tomorrow came to light
Dreams merged to touch the waking mind
Night lost in an array of sunshine

Nothing's been the same since when
You shared my thought and soul
The walls to awareness leveled
By a simple truth bestowed

*

176

Are we conscious of the thoughts we share
The pattern that builds our molecules
A blueprint theme and variations
Of the force that weaves our beings
Together?

*

177.

We stand behind evolution
Waiting our place in the line
Of feet-on-the-ground creature motion
Envious of those in flight

Size and weight, metals and plastic
We've engineered home and hearth
With furniture and appliances
Along paths of concrete and tar

Possessions should be tools
Not burdens to hold us back
But used to speed our work
The weight of a treasure subtracts from its worth

We enter life universal
And attempt to express our potential
Little birds are angels
If we listen they'll lighten our hearts

*

178.

Once I had a home of hope
Safe and comfortable
But that was lifetimes ago

Harshness and hate
Where there is no trust
Pain fights pain

The winner delivers first thrust
Kindness is misinterpreted as such
And compassion dies in the dust

And decays and disintegrates
And disappears into the soul
Where love forgot to grow
I need a quiet place to heal
From the poison that made me ill
Where I can breathe

I know not if it is safe to feel
Should ugliness be concealed
If it cannot be exterminated?

Cover it up
Or expose it to be isolated
And protect the victims wrongly hated
Who have nowhere else to go

To escape the pettiness
And find how to belong
Sensitivity and depth are grown
In secret in the soul

*

179.

Across the green grass crystals
And inside the mighty wood
A tiptoeing shadow
Passed over your lawn
And over your whisper I stood

Out from the stardust window
And down from the cotton cloud belt
A faint shadow gliding
Breezed over your lawn
And under your bloomed bush I knelt

While mighty shapes encircled
The pink haven butterfly loft
A pink blossom drifted
Down onto your lawn
And into my palm felt soft

*

180.

Paula was a good friend
Accepted without thought
It's hard to judge escapism
In one who never found fault

*

117

181.

Expectation is coincidence
Creation of all incidents
Suspicion closes doors and vents
And feelings are suppressed
Under tremendous pressure

Matter gives way under stress
Mistrust creates accidents
But when feelings are expressed
All there is supports the balance
As fresh air rushes in

Secrets are kept
To protect
The one within

*

182.

Orphaned by a loveless freedom
Rejected by countless fetters
I have become absorbed in depth
And adopted by the universe

What a strange fate and yet
Merely destiny of all
To flow like a river into the ocean
And merge with the parent of creation

*

183.

All things dead
Come to life
When spirit enters

It is energy
Entering mass
Taking shelter for a night

Taking part in the dream
When we see the good in the bad
We are free

Secrets no longer exist
With the ability
To transmit

Being out of form
Into form
And out again

*

184.

I thought I had the answers yesterday
But they were only questions
I could have opened all the doors
Today I have the reasons

Your nightmares shape my wandering thought
I stand before another lock
A world of days with no dark fears
Tomorrow has no clock

Colors of the future shape my daydreams
Stars rise in tomorrow's sky
Closed doors are walls when locked by our confusion
But we own the key to why

Tomorrow seems so lost and far away
We pass through every season
Shutting doors not used today
In logic without reason

Forever seems so lost and far away
We stand before the answers
Eternity verses today
Love and truth are forever

*

185.

Day after day feeling verses fact
All of the pain obliterates tact
And feelings get hurt

There's no easy way
Polarities reverse
Result's the same
Relationships break

Oversimplify and try to understand
Without fixing blame
Do what I can

Interminable plight vexes and traps
Creates rejection
Discrimination and overt selection
Undoes bonding
Infers perfection is a possibility

Unrealistic expectation
The story of my life
Tolerance to the point of breaking
Implies another side

Hidden in a dark abscess of mind
Indiscretion yet reveals
The consummate test of time

What is struggling to break through
To see the light of day
Defensive criticism shields indestructible grace
Fragile beauty waiting still
In its hiding place

Effortless composure
Mythological beast
Wrestles with my conscience
And yet defies release

It's all a matter of control
I never do succeed
Wanting someone to pay attention
Endorphins drown in substance P

While no one seems to listen to me
Withdraw, recant, recede
Energy battles exhaustion
In daily pursuit of peace

It's like tending a garden
Knowing when to weed
And being attacked by mosquitoes
And swarms of killer bees

The nervous system is in control
Will succumbs to disease
The best intentions meet their deaths
Drowning in neural seas

If attitude builds thought patterns
Layer upon layer
Peeled back show disturbance
That got me off track

Derailed by my denial
Of something inside me
Denial of my own
Oversensitivity

No one knows how long we have
To compound our mistakes
Indulging in false remedies
Until the dreamer wakes

*

186.

Noise shatters the soul's window
Piercing the stillness of the pond
With shards of shattered glass
Distorting and rippling the reflective surface
Only to blend and disappear
In stillness recomposed

*

187.

The brain is the umbilical cord of the dreamer
Deep in the heart we make a connection
It's with the dreamer in others we find contentment

Bring the right vibration
Into conscious realization
And you won't be disappointed

*

188.

Time is a toy
We climb ever higher
For a moment of joy
On a mountain of pain

My eyes grow weaker
My heart breaks again
And I feel so unwanted
By the world

Life is charades
But I don't know the game
Misplaced in time
Trying to find a friend

I have to laugh
To hide humiliation
Life must be funny
To be so degrading

It takes your love
And steals your dreams
And I feel so unwanted
By the world

*

189.

How easy it is to depend on pleasures
Needing to feel good above all else
Searching them out takes so much time
But other than hurt, what else?

Television numbs the senses
Ice cream and chocolate ease the pain
Conversation would help but it's dangerous
Who to trust?

And the doctor comes along
And takes away the medicine
Left with the ultimate addiction
I breathe in and out once again

*

190.

Profound sadness
Extreme disappointment
Inexplicably hapless
Miscreant disanointed
Unbound madness
Priorities disjointed

Experimental dances
Beyond the coded norm
We took our chances
Maybe it isn't good form
But none seem to outlast
Chaos of the storm

We search for happiness
It changes form
Until we find at last
The eye of the storm
Where creation rests
And we are unharmed

*

191.

It's a wonder more people don't just disappear
Overwhelmed by a flood of events
In trying to sort it all out
We awaken dormant fears

Disappear into a different way
Something wakes up inside
The highways we build are distant echoes of dreams
Memories of desires we seek

We are not forgetful
But disappear to the world
Still knowledge is timeless
The inner projected without

*

192.

We think we have to think to grow
But thought is projection
While learning is reception

So often thinking blocks what we know
And only by revealing reason
Is the truth exposed

*

193.

The wisdom of the soul
Sleeps within our cells
Waking in the dead of night
In the darkness a spark of light
The flash of electricity we call life

We see ourselves as sleeping mass
Mirrors don't lie
They reverse the truth
And energy flows in the wrong direction
Until we smash the image that confuses

*

194.

Until my lost friend came back
There was only a key in a book
And now I see a universe
Hidden by failure to look

To some an adventure
To some barrier
To some just water for chores

But another's character
Won't change the river
Any more than a rock on the shore

*

195.

It's ok to be myself
I'm already good enough
Rejecting me was their mistake
I can't give them an excuse to love

It's not my fault they scream and yell
It doesn't matter to them if I cry
They don't listen to me anyway
Arguing is a waste of time

I'm not responsible for what others think
I'm not responsible for being ignored
If I'm me no one will love me less
Telling the truth can't hurt any more

*

196.

I don't have feathers
I don't have wings
But a little bluebird
Taught me to sing

Underneath
The confusion of words
Joy springs
From simplicity

I was charmed from the start
She rearranged my days
And left wings on my heart
When she flew away

*

197.

Physical perception rises and evolves
Into individual personification
That only finds happiness when allowed
To be

Perception from within
That does not depend
On anything external
Is happy

*

198.

There is life beyond these frail bodies
I don't know if we're meant to see
But you have brightened the light in me

Poets and artists always seem to suffer
The pain of their boundaries
For the enlightenment or entertainment of others

But pain cannot survive us
Nor can apathy
Time is the body's burden

And spirit is light
It knows a geological age as a day
And sees endless rainbows in the pouring rain

*

199.

Imagine what your world would be like
If you were the only one of your kind
Or if all others were simple-minded
Looking to you for guidance

And what if the genesis of the universe
Was there prepared to reverse your senses
And flow out to touch those simple-minded
Ready to receive it?

The greatest words are left unspoken
Hidden but written in the heart

*

200.

Why spend a day a week
Kneeling in front of an icon
When our noblest purpose is
To witness all creation?

*

201.

That friend of mine was close to me
But she wasn't close to herself
She wasn't afraid to frighten me
By trying to kill herself

I can't reach her—maybe none can
Cause she still has to reach herself
But I suspect she knows what she's done
By her cries and her screams of hell

I tried to reach her—to touch her life
But I couldn't catch hold of her
So shrill is the voice of that wretched life
That I'll try not to think of her

So speak a gentle word to me
Help me quiet the noise
Whisper something gentle and sweet
And use your kindest voice

That acquaintance I've only just met
Is confused and needs advice
But I've none to give and I still can't forget
An old friend's hopeless cries

I need someone to comfort him
And show him where to turn
I need someone to answer him
And cool what could easily burn

But who will he listen to
If he can't hear himself?
How can he accept someone new
If he can't accept himself?

So speak a gentle word to me
Say you'll hold out your hand
To grasp whatever comes peacefully
And touch me if you can

And this pair of eyes—you're dear to me
But I don't think you know it yet
So while you're here stay near to me
Maybe you can help me forget

You've seen just how confused I am
I've watched you lose yourself
But I've grown weak and you're still strong
Please help me help myself

I'd like to help and encourage you
To be a gentle man
I don't want the same thing to happen to you
That happened once to an old friend

So speak a gentle word to me
Show me you understand
That when you need love you can turn to me
Speak as softly as you can

*

202.

How could anyone look at the sky
And say there's nothing there?
How could anyone look in your eyes
And say you don't care?

I questioned your thoughts that I could not see
Till the world of your mind had come to me
I chose to go where we'd been before
As I entered the room you held open the door

No need for either
To be left in the dark
You follow your mind
I'll follow my heart

*

203.

Listen closely to the movement of life
That embroiders the under depths of the world
Stranded to be captured beyond the ear's grasp
So gentle and subtle when first it is heard
Until awareness grows of this intricate word

Ingeniously interwoven patterns of vibration
Soon have mounted to the heights of thunderous roar
And subside as quickly as you turn your mind
To some meaningless menial chore

It's all perception
The key is perception
So do what you've done before
With awareness
And listen

Somewhere in the depths of your unconscious
The complicated syncopated patterns of existence
Are alive
And wait to come to your senses

*

204.

Every day is a new beginning
The birds wake up and sing
Announce the wonders the day is bringing
Little Emma sings

Every moment is its own story
Welcome each partner for dancing
No matter the beat or intricacy
Emma is always happy

And in the silence that stills her heart
The peace that forces us to part
The trills of her voice still thrill my being
Emma sweetly sings to me

Little Emma wise and happy
Accepts me as I am
Always greets me—happy to see me
Never tried to pretend

Except when she was suffering
She tried to hide the pain
An angel who could only bring joy
Emma was my best friend

*

205.

The mystery of life
Is the way we live
The mystery's unsolved
As long as we exist

In delusion of fantasy
What we don't admit
Veils the external world

The mystery's disease
Riddles us to death
Before the body fails

And mocks us in our ignorance
Of nervousness and energy
That mutinies and makes us sick
Until we wake up and be

*

206.

I thought I'd put the pain behind
And then you said my name
It doesn't make sense anymore
The feeling's not the same

I put it aside
It hurt too much
To know you wouldn't share
You led me on

You'll do it again
I still believe you care
But when it comes down to the truth
You're never there

You always say you're waiting for me
I step forward and you retreat
I'm no longer crawling, begging or wishing
If you want me come and get me

Cause love is more than superficial emotion
It's the courage to be
As far as I can see
There's no one here but me

Your words are pretty
Your thoughts are nice
We were good together
Your heart is mine

But I can't live your life
And you rejected mine
Maybe someday
Maybe sometime

Can't count on maybe
To fulfill a life
No doubt you inspired me
In giving direction have been kind

But by our own choice we can only share spirit
Cause you wouldn't share the fears and limits
That have built my universe
And I won't bring my pain home to you

But know forever my courage to be
Grew by you reaching out to me
As I know even when you're not there
You care

The pain is just too much to bear
But still it strengthens me
When you look at me
Is it me you see?

*

207.

Where there is love it can be channeled
To anyone anywhere
Where there is human there is love of some kind
For the universe to share

To limit my love to one
Deprives me of some hidden sun
That someone else holds in his mind

To limit ourselves to some
Deprives us of some hidden love
Buried in the vastness of mankind

*

208.

Defense is natural
It's supposed to defend
But when it can't comprehend
Why all the suffering—

Accidental friendly fire
Unintentional stress increase
Adrenaline needs to be released
But someone locked the door

Cause no one's listening
No one's there
Everyone's deafened by war
So defend

Inflammation of connective tissue
I guess I'm just coming unglued
Nothing around me makes sense anymore
Why should this be new?

Autoimmune disorder
Exhausted needing comfort
In a chaotic world
I surrendered

*

209.

We look up for guidance
But the river runs down
As we backtrack to its source

Fill the cup
Follow the course
Passing us by
When we look up

The source is like ice
But all the wonders along the way
Are worth the price

*

210.

The mind is a selfish child
That demands attention constantly
The heart is an easy fellow
Content to work without recognition

Lack of emotion
Is the ultimate privation

And when the mind is troubled
And working overtime
The heart says take it easy

*

211.

Duality
Is the contradiction of our world
The basic need to be free
Of choices lost to habit

Choice requires rejection
Of anything not chosen
And mourning of the loss
The death of unpicked options

Routine is the skeleton
On which we hang our pleasure
Our natural delight hangs in suspense
Of changes immeasurable

When openness allows quiet penetration
Influence succeeds in ego dissolution
When force of character alone influences
One leaves the problem to become solution

Dark gives light
And light infinite color
And then we try to formalize
And see a rigid pattern

I fly on white wings
And let moonlight shine through me
All light and sound
Are waves that bear me

Past the world of boundaries
Decision is the intersection
Of danger and opportunity
An invitation to feast on creation

Confront the infinite
And confront the worst
Paradox
Is the structure of the universe

*

212.

So many words wasted
As info overload
I revel in the silence
Of feelings yet untold

Too soon becoming memories echoed
Whispers in the cold
Vast darkness between the glittering stars
The spaces between souls

*

213.

The air that crept inside
Flowed out once again
Separating thoughts from body
Letting the essence
Flow through momentarily

In time we come to see all sides
Realizing commonality
Shadows from the reflected light
Dance delightfully
As the moon sets opposite the dawn
It doesn't matter what bodies we put on

*

214.

Electricity flows peacefully
Through my body
Pores opened to open air

Breath mingles with the breeze
Hidden in the mist of stillness
Apparent nothingness
Pours love and light through being

*

215.

Cold water bubbling
Out of mountaintop snows
Lower down a river flows
Over green, blue and purple
Rambling through lush vegetation
Above a bouquet of summer colors
Downy snow shines and glistens
Of fresh water from frozen shores

Snow in early June
Enough to block the roads
Orange and pink adobe bricks
Built into a cliff
Where a community once made its home

The sun sets over the ceremonial pit
And shows the entrance
Where the spirit of the cliff
Came out and danced
And wept where a river now flows

*

216.

In the red haze of sunset
We are burning stars on crossed paths
Colliding into one at day's end

Now you have drifted from me as I watch
Your thoughts sparkle like starlight
And touch me in the dark

In the yellow glow of fireflies
We are dancers of the twilight
Swallowed by the darkness to be lost

But if we keep the rhythm no one hears
We can feel the motion
Even in the dark

In the blue of forever
We are two flying lovers
Angels in the heaven of our souls

Touching the horizon turns to gold
And morning flows
Day's river of afterglow

*

217.

Static electricity leads to burnout
Thunder clears the air for peace
Friction buildup caused by tension
Needs release

Strain of trying to force
Makes muscles lock and vision blur
Just see
Accept and be

*

218.

A being of awareness
Of eternal peace
Passes quickly through the world

An intangible fortress of universal balance
Keeps us entranced in this world
Till momentary distraction

Interrupts life
I have no eternity
Just a moment in time

*

219.

What a holy place is a garden
That the butterfly should visit there
What a holy place is human
That love should strike so often there

Love abides where beauty dwells
Holy is sin when God visits hell
For all our apathy and airs
The God in us seems to be everywhere

*

220.

I've stood upon your shore before
It was a sheltered port
Being at odds across the water
Gives me little comfort

The rhythmic flow of poetry
The beating of the heart
The rise and fall upon the beach
Of the pounding surf

The crest and ebb of ocean swells
I am adrift upon
Fall inside the wake you left
I drift now that you're gone

The sea is full of wonder
It sings the song of peace
As I pen verse to paper
I am now floating free

*

221.

As the seasons pass
And each year ends
While little else lasts
We'll always be friends

*

222.

It's all an energy crisis
Energy to focus on reality is needed
To concentrate on the nature of being

It's frightening to acknowledge similarity
With criminals, wastrels, liberals and Nazis
Intolerance is dread of change

The work of butterflies is beauty
To play and flutter and court each other
They don't need crime or incivility

As we look at ourselves with pity and reverence
So much to be learned from honesty
Cowardice is nothing to run away from

*

223.

To whom it may concern
I'd hoped by now to learn
How not to scare people away

I seem to have disappeared
In the heart that I held dear
I didn't know my place

Rejection my worst fear
Outside among my peers
Ignored in chronic shame

If no one sees your tears
You cry but no one hears
Do you still feel the pain?

*

224.

A summer dawn in the little hills
Reams of pale grass under looming forebodance
Kindness in the land but not the sky
And all is gentle to the eye

Now the spaces have opened as clouds condense
Sent to the horizon in turbulence
As a funnel of destruction clears a path
Stirring the countryside to dance

Country music blares in the restaurant
Everywhere songs are about somewhere else
The cows asleep in the wet pasture land
Know nowhere else

*

225.

So many different faces
On the Earth today
So many places reachable
By so many ways

Ever has the sun shone
So many different hues
Never have I seen the world
From so many views

Since you took me by the hand
And led me through the skies
You opened up your life
Now I see through your eyes
And you through mine

So many different waves
Along the ocean floor
So many seas above us
We are at the door

Particles in passing
Travel through our bodies
Energies we haven't seen
Constitute our being

Since we are unconscious
Of what makes our minds
You opened up your life
Now I see through your eyes
And you through mine

Yesterday the sky was small
And unreachable
Now it travels on forever
Worlds beyond our walls

Galaxies are flowers
Waiting for the bees
Crawling on the stems of thought
Waiting for the breeze

To lift us to our rendezvous
And travel through the skies
You opened up your life
Now I see through you eyes
And you through mine

*

226.

One cannot attract by repelling
One cannot find love by demanding
Religions are vines rooted in humans
Growing toward the light

Killer kudzu, poison ivy
Honeysuckle and morning glory
The truth is us
Flowers of one bush

*

227.

Twirling blankets of dust
Eat the horizon
Xenophytes in their way
An understatement—everything's overdone
Succulents, scrub and sun

A bleached orphan skeleton
Lies where it died
Overwhelmed by an awesome sky

*

228.

The wonder of what it might be like
To know a mother's love—
Unconditional, noncompetitive
Peaceful coo of dove
In this lifetime I'll never know

Some think the body ultimate
Over death of the soul
Some think life more important
I think them very cold

A child born in rejection pain—
God is not so cruel
But man is a sadist
And woman is a fool

*

229.

Trying to stay busy
To not notice being lonely
Significance recedes

Stormy weather blows
Through the window
Numb and cold

Shuffles my papers about
As I ponder the flame
The wind blew out

The timelessness of dust
Spattered by the rain
To be absorbed as mud

Am I willing to risk
Contact with others
Or am I afraid of the mud?

After being let down so much
I reach out an open hand to touch
But the wind has gone again

Whispering breeze
Over hardened rock
Tempering extremes

Secrets on the wind
Of eternal balance
Begin again in the end

*

230.

Thank you for listening and being with me
I open my heart for you to see
Just another human being

And for all I do differently
While we respect each other's feeling
No difference comes between us

We can be simplistic about this
In simplicity is greatness
And friendship

Touching the basic common essence
The river flows through all of us
It's so simple if we don't pretend
To be different

*

231.

I can't look back
I can't look forward
I can only see here and now
And I'm tired

A rest would seem to be in order
Turn the senses off
Bored to death with pain and pleasure
Turn the whole world off

And let me rest
No more taunting dreams
That never will come true
Just peace

And the yogis tell us how
While society drowns them out
Afraid unless their hearts should beat
They'd be lost

Which way out?
Which way peace?
All I see is me

*

232.

Will you remember the days we spent
Together passing time
Chasing trucks and butterflies
Whispers of notes lost on the breeze
When all the world was green
Will you remember me?

Will you remember counting ships
Together sharing life
While the river passed us by
Clusters of chords lost in the city
In blues and harmony
Will you remember me?

Faces find their way through time
Forgetting, sleeping, dreaming
Memories are buried alive
Flickering, shining, dimming

*

233.

Once I had a piece of your life
You had a piece of mine
You laid me down and walked away
I guess you changed your mind

Once I had a piece of your heart
Now I don't have the time
I don't know when the sharing stopped
And I don't know why

Once you had a piece of me
Now we pretend not to care
But somewhere deep the feeling hides
Let's just admit it's there

Maybe in another world
We could try again
Come by my neighborhood someday
You know I'll let you in

*

234.

When you know you are equal with everyone
You've soared above prejudice
When you know you're the same as each grain of sand
There is no love on Earth you can miss
When you know you're one with death and the rain
Your love will reach beyond hate
Beyond pain

*

235.

I want to believe what I hear
The tone has a twist of luck
But after rationalizing fear
I just hear what I want to trust

Somewhere inside beats the heart of a child
That's screaming to be free from doubt
Since I lost my innocence
Being burned more than once

*

236.

Leave me my delusion
Of this there is no doubt
That any lesson left unlearned
Is bound to come back round

Love is the great illusion
The Goddess claims her own
I must draw this conclusion
The Goddess lives alone

She is the drummer and the band
The dancer and the beat
She is the lover and the man
Who trembles at her feet

The mystery has unfolded
A simple naked truth
The evidence discloses
Eternity for proof

And thus performance closes
There is no place on Earth
Where satisfaction poses
I must abandon search

And leave illusory domicile
For peace so deep beyond
With distant starlight reconcile
And thus I must abscond

*

237.

Unspoken words
Also unwritten
Remain hidden

*

238.

A missing piece of the past
A mystery clear as glass
Solution should be obvious
But generations ask

Numbers do not lie
But do we understand
The methods that apply
When all have lost the plan?

*

239.

What manner of desperation
Drives someone to cheat?
What manner of insecurity
Can make someone believe
A living being is worthless?
Those who choose to destroy life
Live a lie

*

240.

Music is ancient
Dancing is human
Humor is hope

But men make religions
Try to outlaw
The spirit's expression

They have no purpose
Only hate
And mortal bodies

*

241.

I cannot speak for others
But I must speak for myself
Talent comes from practice
And one must practice well

It rises from repression
And fear of being heard
Fear of repercussion
Has led to what I've learned

And now it is compulsion
I'll never be silent again
Even in seclusion
I exercise my pen

*

242.

Inside my private fantasy
There's nothing between you and me
No danger to my self-esteem
Just an open hand and space to breathe

The wind doesn't care
The sky is complete
I'm free to love
And you care about me

Then reality calls my name
The lift of experience going down
No one else is calling me
Silence is a lonely sound

But even silence vibrates
Stillness reveals energy
Within completeness needing nothing
An essence of totality

And I believe what I hear
I hear what I want to hear
Turn an ear to creation
And just be

*

243.

Words come forth expressing potential
In appreciation of the emptiness of a page
Because it can be filled

Or a goblet of tears
That can be spilled
And emptied in evaporation

If it doesn't exist
It has or it will
Will is life potential

Emergence sprouting power
A bud never opened
Is an eternal flower

*

244.

Out of the north
Kind breezes blow freely
Licking bright butter gold fronds
As oil pumps keep rhythm
Hearts beating the passing time
Open spaces
Muted places blown by
A timeless sky

Windmills spinning in the fields
Of bouncing and bobbing golden reels
Wild flowers dancing with the clouds
With eternity in the sun pouring down

*

245.

Is it possible to exist
Without constant disappointment?
I see those who thrive on it

Unable to dive
Barely skimming the surface
They trample fools like me

And were it not for the constant kicking
Of feet unable to reach the bottom
I would think me of use to no one

They poke around amid the coral
Ignoring what lies in the depths below
Why should they care?

Life will go on tomorrow
Eternity will always be there

                                    *

246.

Sunshine and rainbows
And cotton ball clouds
I look through my window
And want you here now

But your world is winter
You're trapped by the snow
Waiting for the summer sun
To show you where to go

Red leaves and snowflakes
And Christmas tree lights
Memories are painful
We're buried in time

But beauty's the secret
To let the sun shine
Till the truth is seen
In your world and mine

Moonshine and starlight
You are your dreams
We are the daylight
Doubt shadows between

All we need do
Is believe
And follow our dreams
Follow your dreams

*

247.

Duality thrives on opposites
Perfect balance is a bore
And thus minority dissension
Is required to encounter scorn

It's all opinion anyway
The fact is that we are
Emotional and indiscreet
In wishing others harm

The point is that a stranger
A wanderer from beyond
Has landed here and learned to fear
What others reckon on

*

248.

Afloat like a chain of islands
We only skim the surface
If you go ashore I will follow

Like a pebble standing still in time
Against the forces of the clime
Dry spot in the depth of brine

Imprints remain
Where pebbles fall
When we are gone
An impression is all

But enough to impact
At least from the surface
A memory imprint
A hint of purpose

Beautiful gifts
Are found in the holes
Where from over high cliffs
Small pebbles fall

*

249

I've spent so many words
And time is passing on
Flowers bloom again each year
Clouds disperse to reap new forms

I cannot say all that I feel
Or would we too disperse?
Then maybe it's time for thoughts to bloom
And reshape what is real

All our time is like a dream
To work so close we live as one
Spirals grow as symbiotically
We ever echo love

I cannot touch all that you feel
In time I'll come to know
Through dreams caress what is innermost
And restate what is real

I cry in stained glass tears
The cloudburst clears the sky
And dissipates my fears
And lets the spirals rise

The colored drops reflect the sun
Within me
For never is it not enough
To simply be

*

250.

Left behind fragments
Of my decaying past
Under dark waters
In the swamps of the past
Sunk to the bottom and broken apart
Into tiny pieces
All that's worth keeping floats to the surface
Now reassembled and re-emerging
At last

*

251.

I trespass silently
On a white burial ground
Where over the centuries
Treasures lost and found

Drift in and out of consciousness
Holy ground where life is born
Leave behind your outer shell
As you cross over

Lapping tones vocal
In a rhythm strange to me
Deposit remnant discarded shells
On the churning beach

A multitude of ripples
Converge to surge the surf
And play in patterns on the sand
That sifts through open fingers

As in the rhythm of the tide
Trickle down the sands of time
Dropping the departed there
Where I find buried treasure

*

252.

All I am to you is words on a page
But I have a body that needs to be touched
I have a spirit that needs to feel loved
I have a broken heart

Every time I try to pick up the pieces
Someone knocks them out of my hand
And scatters and shatters whatever is left
I have a pile of sand

I'd like a broom to sweep it away
And forget it ever happened
There is rhythm in being beaten
But rhyme has crumbled

*

253.

The essence of pure earthiness
Beyond description in physical terms
Spoken in the stillness of opening petals—

The intensity of emotion in the actor's expression
As he stands alone on the stage
In a desperate silent outcry

Of the hopelessness in which he is engaged
To entrance a senseless audience
Into his world

*

254.

I watched the corn pop
On the stalk
While black crows mocked
And scarecrows talked

About the trivia of the day
And prosperity seems so far away
When you don't know what you need
To be happy

*

255.

Enclosed in a bubble
Unable to touch
Life is a mirror

Reflecting the trouble
Image as such
Creates a barrier

Ever so fragile
So easy to shatter
This protective wrapper

So risky
So frightening
So lonely

*

256.

How many ages
Have we stood apart
And looked across the waves
Pondering alone our thoughts

And I am petrified
In isolation
Sometimes terrified
Of the distance

So much frustration
Doubt in the silence
Waiting for the sound
To breathe again

*

257.

There's a time for growth
And for dormancy
A lifetime in every acorn
And a year in every leaf

In crumbling a leaf
I hold the mystery
Of old age in my young hand

Eternity is found
In such things as brown leaves

*

258.

Musty sky about to rain
Intermittent showers all day
So humid my skin would never dry here
Short-sighted rolling countryside
Infinite shades of color green
Susans smile gold with chocolate eyes
So many worlds lost in the kudzu ivy
Interwoven tiger lilies and Queen Anne's lace
Play in the shadow of woodland grace
Pressed against a lightning studded sky—
I saw it strike near the deer crossing

Topless trees where a tornado once passed
Shed innocent pine scent as if nothing happened
This country maze of wilderness paradise
Led me to town for an hour or so
Where I learned the cotton's been ruined this year
By too many rainbows

*

259.

Everyone a little snowflake
Everyone a little life
Everyone a little heartache
Everyone a little mind

Everyone a little different
Everyone a different size
Everyone a little instant
Everyone a different time

Everyone a different problem
Everyone a different smile
Everyone a different emblem
Everyone a different style

Everyone a different hang-up
Everyone a little kind
Everyone a little rush
Everyone a little behind

Everyone a different voice
Everyone a different hum
Everyone a little choice
Everyone a different sum

Everyone a different right
Everyone a little wrong
Everyone a different light
Everyone a little song

Everyone a little winter
Everyone a different day
Everyone a little summer
Everyone a different way

Everyone a little feeling
Everyone a little word
Everyone a different meaning
Everyone a different world
Everyone a little friendship
Everyone a different love
Everyone a little magician
Everyone a different touch

Everyone a little teardrop
Everyone a little strife
Everyone a little snowflake
Everyone a little life

*

260.

Wisdom eludes the habit of death
The trifles of words at the graveside are stilled
Accept yourself as a creature of wealth
And claim your birthright of will

Threads of all run through the race
The simple smile, the basic face
The memorable scent of a human flower
Will linger beyond its name

*

261.

Fly to the sun and burn your wings
Or spin in the vortex of love
Fear is a gravity
Fly to the center
Come back to me

I can't give up on you
Love is a road that goes forward in time
We can't go back
But we'll always have time
And I can't give up on you

Yesterday we stood on the beach
Today there's an ocean between us
Fear is a gravity
Walk on the water
Come back to me

I can't give up on you

*

262.

Step into my forest
And gently take a leaf
Maybe care enough to share
A piece of earth with me

For all my shyness
Show me patience
And I will love you more

*

263.

Everyone's dream is their own
No one dream can live alone
The rights of the past are tomorrow's wrong
Unless every dream can grow

I choose my friends as I please
I know where I belong
Your boat may sail different seas
I need not go where you've gone

The great minds of all time
Love beyond what they can see
But their lives are spent in a constant fight
To live as they choose to be

And they tell us to love each other
They say freedom is our right
But we stifle the beat of the different drummer
And the right to protest for right

Where would we be if those great men
Had been free from the beginning—
If we could listen instead of hating them
How much more the loving?

And if you live differently
I will not question your right to love
The greater your freedom then surely will be
The greater your gift of love

*

264.

Old river boats
Hauling their freight
In time wear down
Of their own weight

But the river flows on

*

265.

To be the words one tries to speak
The thought one cannot say
The stairway I would try to raise
If I but knew the way

And all the waves in air and sea
Are lines connecting you and me
Draw for me a self-portrait
With the world's lines of suns and skies

Thank you for the flowers
For the fragile smile of life

In between the clouds and fields
We drift inside a dream
As if our thoughts could capture us
And tell us what to be

And all the songs we have set free
Are songs of love of you and me
Sing of all the love there is
In all of time and all above

Thank you for the flowers
For your gentle touch of love

To be the songs one tries to sing
The dream one cannot say
The gateway I would gladly make
If I but knew the way

And all the days we have to be
Are time connecting you and me
Tell me of the worlds you'd share
With thought waves at your fingertips

Thank you for the flowers
For the stars you could not pick

*

266.

Confusion is trying to read too much into
Illusion is needing nonessentials
Transcend complication

Rise above restrictions
Of illusion of limitation
Of confusion

Pebbles for skipping
Pebbles for sunning
Pebbles for just lying around

*

267.

Counting sheep to help me sleep
Number eight had wings
That gentle lamb—my woolly friend
Chased me in my dreams

High on a mountain top one night
A billy goat nudged me and I fell
And landed on a soft wool bed
Of love and peace safe and well

Swimming in the ocean deep
Deafening calm within
A fish with glasses spoke to me
Afraid to even swim

Now I could see just blurs at best
Of ripples in the sunless current
But this wise fish could love far more
And bring the sun into the depths

When I awoke I had grown wings
Butterfly in blue
My woolly love now silver dove
Sang until I knew

We cannot see until we feel
What everyone dreams and thinks is real
Amid the glittering song of doves
The continuous drone of love

*

268.

An innocent bubble blown into the air
Silent and delicate
Try to hear it

It rises on a current of air
Spinning
Catch it on a stick
For a second I hold a feeling for beauty I always will
        hold
Soap made a bubble for just a few seconds
How pointless

*

269.

We grow up sheltered in our minds
Seriously wrong or right
When life is just a joke
Waiting for the punch line

Awestruck we explore our world
Believing what we see
Myths and legends and explanations
We faithfully believe

The joke is on us
Disease of the unconscious
Manifest in suffering
It's all so serious

The problem must be identified
Explored and understood
Before the solution can be clear
An external projection appears

A myth, a fairy tale
A riddle with a key
Symbolic even mystical
Projected externally

Reduces down into a pattern
Internal chemistry
The answer is transmitted
By our own electricity

*

270.

Someday when I pass over
I want no one to suffer for me
I would permit no indignity
Nor wailing cry

But the timeless music from a songbird's throat
Passing by in the breeze
Like an oracle to echo
One's unconscious thought

Flown away from this world
Like the passing of a dream
Blended into the peace of the blessed
Al a bama—here may we rest

*

271.

Once in the starry glint of night
The mystic mirror met my gaze
And masked my sight in moonlit haze

While sinking in a mire of pain
The hand of hope held fast to mine
And held me bathed in Hestia's wine

In the aura of explosive surge
We merged in holographic flame
And what it did to me and you
Is left for others to explain

Fire consumes and melts away
And leaves an empty void where pain
Once preoccupied the soul—
The heart a million miles away

Humor's the stuff of materialization
We're clowns—echoes of divine
Experience scripts future intention
In the light of laughter love's light shines

Once in the darkest depths of despair
I was caught in your hunter's lair
And all that mattered was you were there

The symmetry of duality's prose
You were captured where I froze
The dance is spinning in the wind
Our song an echo in the din

Still I stop every once in a while
To recapture that magical moment's mood
But all that matters must evolve
I get the joke—do you?

*

272.

From sand reclaimed from the salt of the sea
Land between the tides
Over the beaches a steady breeze
Reaches across from the other side
In rhythmic pulse that soothes the soul
Days pass in patterns ruled by the moon
And reflections of deep dreams unfold

*

273.

I was set up from the start
An outcast with a broken heart
How dare you ridicule the dreams
We shared in the world of in betweens

This road has come to an end
No one to inherit, no one to befriend
A useless occupation of space
A mistranslation of the human race

I worked so hard to embrace hope
But it's dangerous to trust what you do not know
Blind faith is stupidity run amuck
It leaves you exposed like a sitting duck

Others seem to know the rules of the game
I thought I'd figure it out along the way
The worst part is finding my feelings don't matter
To those who have hurt me the most

I know to you I'm just stumbling
But I can't seem to work it all out
Leaving solitude is gambling
That I might survive the next bout

I dare to think and philosophize
In the dark with flooding eyes
Rejection invites suicide
To avoid believing in lies

Suffering is eternity
Until bliss blindly defies
Dissolves the angst and misery
Vanquished in a flick of time

*

274.

Beautiful words in a sea of daisies
All in the darkness—the moon of a dream
The words all a mystery, an echo, a plea
Songs of a blind flower—the gentle weed

Whispered to men she could see through the skies
And dance on the cloudless beach of time
Her wings are music as the wind flies
Knowing time through the seed in a daisy's eye

Animals stuffed in the dark age of war
With radio parts the sound waves were torn
The strings of the harp sound like a mirror
Reflecting the peace of long before

When daisies sang at night in the garden
The war then was far from home
The strings of the harp are long abandoned
Finding the jewel of the nightless poem

Innocent games stir the blood of men
Where trust is dissolved the anger steps in
But time turns its wheels as the tide shuffles sands
And tomorrow washes up on the beach again

Weather-tossed and denouncing the nations
We draw the borders soul to soul
No one has not suffered, died or lost
Wildflowers will always grow

*

275.

Moose and maples
A mass of color
In fluorescent foliage
Naked beauty
Everywhere the eye can see

Maze of woodland
Along mystery's lakes
In silver and gold
Nature's levels layered
Each revealing the soul

Mostly in between
Allegory and metaphor
It's simple simile
Natural rapport
Explains life as a dream

*

276.

Love has more substance than matter itself
The substance of God
The body of life
Within the reality of the animal mind

Within the totality—the eternity of time
Two people in love embrace all there is
As they encounter a world of limits
That cannot exceed the material

There is no power greater than love
No other force capable exists
To unite those parted by physical forms

Neither man nor words nor law
Can pronounce the reality of love—
Only God

Inside the awareness of the human mind
Is the key to the mystery of God
People in love can encompass creation
And exceed the material world's limitations
To unite separate particles in a single wavelength
And be one

Neither man nor words nor law
Can pronounce the reality of God—
Only love

*

277.

I am no longer rapt with me
The world has lost its magic
Mystique now wrapped tight in a shroud
Ensnared, entombed and tragic

When did I realize the truth
That love does not empower
But teaches comfort in routine
Mild and sweet from sour

To believe in fantasy
Or cling to the unreal
Days rewound and played again
All spring from just one reel

And shed the faith in promises
That died like dried cracked skin
To set both feet upon the earth
Once delicate and thin

The pain of joy and sorrow
That overwhelmed me then
Consumed itself till hollow
And faded fallen in

What is left when novelty
Finds no audience
But fresh release of energy's
Quiet shuffling dance

It's only when we take for granted
And stop to close our eyes
It's always what we didn't know
That takes us by surprise

*

278.

A bubble rises from the surf
Wafts on a current of air
Who knows what changes occur
In the sanctity of that tiny world

The violence—the turbulence—
The experience of feeling
We'll mingle once again in the surf
Once the bubble bursts

*

279.

It's quiet now
Not many others remain
So many gone away

The empty city house
Crowds and noise just echoes
And so the era goes

Behind lethargic dreamers
Drown in their own tears
While busy adventure seekers
Trade moments for years

I've just crossed the threshold
Cleansed of others' debt
Now it's quiet

I watch as an observer
Through a two-way mirror
Not needing to be seen
Not caring to be heard

Enigmatic cloud
Obscures this empty house
And it is quiet now

*

280.

Light crept down upon the planet
And split into a rainbow
All the people living
Fissioned from their home

If two colors blend together
Will the rainbow disappear?
The illusion is confusing
But you are really here

And I've seen your private dreams
There are no secrets in the heart
The rainbow fades but never dies
It never falls apart

Light crept down into my darkness
I'm not the first to sneak a peek
Of the splendor salty and sweet
All the people living

I'd like to give up on living prisms
I want the world to be whole
What's the point of seeing visions
If we can't touch the gold?

*

281.

You wonder why the ones you hurt
Have nothing left to say
If you listened really good
You just might know someday
That you're the one who turned an ear
And quietly turned away

Did you think of me as just a rock
Kicked up into your shoe?
If you dropped me by the way
I tried to follow you
Ate the dirt that you turned up
I was there for you

*

282.

As always when the sea gets rough
You have a harbor in my love
Come to me and rest a while
Away from all your troubles

I don't know why people lie
And try to lock up what's inside
Come to me and stay a while
Away from all your sorrows

Imagine a world with no heroes
No dictators and no victims
Envision life with us together
We have harmonies to share

*

283.

Sleep tight, dreamless boy
In a world of dreams and visions
All the friends that you've passed by
Wait now with arms extended
To hold you and remember

Learn to comfort, learn to care
Learn to feel what you are touching
For to trust is to be tender
And what you bruise needs mending
I just need to know you're there
Lullabies tonight
As I watch you with another
And I see myself again
Wait to be cast aside
I listened and responded

Try to comfort, try to care
Understand that you are hurting
For I trusted and was tender
Indifference is crushing
I just want you to be fair

*

284.

We're crazy you know
If anyone could see inside
And know the dreams we create
They'd be crazy too

The normal world is blind
They know inside that dreams are real
But they try to hide
And kill the dreams and dreamers
We're prisoners of the blind

You this crazy cannot hurt
That's why I trust you with my thoughts
We dream the dreams and dig the dirt
That hides the treasures taught

*

285.

Sensitivity is a weakness
Is pure selfishness
Sensitivity is a strength
Is clear perception

*

286.

I came to this secluded place
Sincerely seeking rest
I strive to leave an echo trace
Perceptive and perplexed

Between the dark and dim of sleep
Retreating from the din
I center somewhere vast and deep
To take the total in

And wonder that I was so lost
Not knowing who I am
I tried to be all at a cost
I could not come to spend

When one perceives to such a point
One takes entirely in
A flood of everyone conjoined
And drowns the soul within

And so I settle quietly
While drying out my soul
The waters gradually recede
I am becoming whole

*

287.

I don't have my children
They died before being born
I don't have a lover
Because my soul is torn

But there are lots of children
Who always need more love
And there's a child inside me
She wants to see the sun
Before she dies from your indifference
Your neglect, abuse and harm

I have the seed of life within
She wants to know your warmth
For now she's been awakened
Do you mean to do her harm?

For here you have a friendship
If only you will share
There's a child inside me
And she wants to know you care

*

288.

The lake was like a crystal soul
That whispered the breath of wind
And as the planet turned away
And caused the day to end
The music played my inner voice
And I turned around again

For all the love of all the world
And all the life on earth
Without you I'm alone and lost
We're still witnessing our birth
It whispers in our void of night
And turns us to the truth

*

289.

It's scary to look out at the world
And realize no one's in charge
The captain set the ship adrift
And left each passenger a part
Of the navigational chart
No one will ever solve the puzzle
If we hide what's in our hearts

*

Index of Poems by First Line and Number

I began writing poetry in my sleep when I was a teenager. Eventually I learned to write while conscious. For me it's always been therapy to help me understand my feelings and the often cruel world around me. I've been told my sensitivity is my greatest strength and my greatest weakness—and that's true. I feel a very deep connection to Nature and dream symbolism, so there's an element of the metaphysical in my poems.

The sweet gum tree in Poem #123 was one of my favorite places when I was a teenager. Many years later the tree was cut down when that path became a street called Bradford in Cummings Research Park, Huntsville, Alabama.

The first edition of **Ripples on the Surface** was published as a fund-raiser for women with HIV/AIDS in Uganda through Global Partners for Development. Many women were supplied with pigs for piggeries so they could become self-sufficient. I'm grateful to Global Partners for Development and Alice in Uganda for all the good work they continue to do.

This second edition sends all authors' royalties to a retired school teacher from Alabama. The same is true for my second collection of poetry, **Child of the Universe,** which contains poems from 2006 through 2012. And yes, the third collection is being written.

Poetry is very personal. Thank you for sharing this part of my life.

Also by the Author

Child of the Universe, second collection of poetry

Deception Past, a unique novel of reincarnation and past life identity theft told through Tarot Cards, as those involved learn to resolve betrayal with forgiveness.

Dragonfly Dreams, a romance novel about dreams that connect us, dreams that come true, and dreams that reveal the past. "There are places we can only reach in our dreams while our bodies sleep."

Five Flowers, a novel of five historical Tudor queens who reincarnate as historical characters in Victorian London's Whitechapel district and again as historical characters in the US in the 1960s.

Please visit the author's website at
www.reincarnationbooks.com

Please visit the author's page at
www.IndependentAuthorNetwork.com

Please visit the publisher's page at
www.KatMoranPublications.com

www.ingramcontent.com/pod-product-compliance
Lightning Source LLC
Chambersburg PA
CBHW060237050426
42448CB00009B/1476